Online Community Moderation

A Guide to Handling User-Generated Content

Dr Alex Bugeja, PhD

--

Table of Contents

Introduction

Welcome to the internet's engine room. You may not see the moderators, but you see their work everywhere. Every time you read a helpful product review, participate in a non-toxic discussion about a sensitive topic, find a useful answer in a support forum, or enjoy a competitive but fair online game, you are experiencing the results of effective community moderation. It is the invisible architecture that supports civilized interaction in the sprawling, chaotic, and endlessly creative digital world we inhabit. Without it, the internet as we know it would collapse into a howling vortex of spam, scams, and vitriol. This is not hyperbole; it is the daily reality that moderators push back against.

The explosion of user-generated content, or UGC, has fundamentally reshaped our digital landscape. It is the lifeblood of the modern web, the constant, torrential flow of text, images, videos, and reviews created by users, not by the platforms themselves. This content powers multi-billion dollar social media empires, builds niche communities for every imaginable hobby, and has become the primary way many people discover information and make decisions. Consumers now spend, on average, over five hours a day engaging with content created by their peers. This shift is monumental. Trust has migrated from traditional advertising to peer recommendations, with the vast majority of people trusting online reviews and user content far more than a brand's own marketing.

This reliance on UGC is a double-edged sword. While it fosters authenticity and connection, it also opens the door to a host of problems. The same openness that allows a supportive community to flourish also allows malicious actors to spread disinformation, harass individuals, and post harmful content. The sheer volume is staggering, making any attempt at oversight a monumental task. Platforms must contend with billions of posts, comments, and uploads daily. This isn't just a technical challenge; it's a human one. Every piece of that content represents a person's expression, and deciding where to draw the line between acceptable and unacceptable is one of the most complex and contentious issues of our time.

This is where the practice of online community moderation enters the picture. It is the formal process of monitoring, evaluating, and managing user-generated content to ensure it aligns with a platform's guidelines, community standards, and legal requirements. The primary goal is to foster a safe, constructive, and welcoming environment for users. Think of it as urban planning for a digital city. A well-moderated space has clear rules of the road, public parks for pleasant interaction, and a reliable system for dealing with those who would disrupt the peace. A poorly moderated or unmoderated space quickly descends into anarchy, driving away the very people who make the community valuable in the first place.

This book is a comprehensive guide to that practice. It is designed for anyone who is, or aspires to be, on the front lines of handling user-generated content. Whether you are a professional community manager for a global brand, a volunteer moderator for a passionate fan forum, a startup founder building a new social app, or simply a curious digital citizen who wants to understand how online spaces are governed, this book is for you. We will demystify the processes, strategies, and tools used to create and maintain thriving online communities.

Our journey will be a practical one. We begin with the fundamentals, exploring what an online community truly is and why people are drawn to them. We will lay the groundwork by examining the crucial role of the moderator and the absolute necessity of establishing clear, fair, and enforceable community guidelines. These are the constitutional documents of your digital society, and getting them right is the first and most important step toward building a healthy environment. A community without clear rules is not a bastion of free expression; it is simply a chaotic and unwelcoming space where the loudest and most aggressive voices dominate.

From there, we will dive into the day-to-day work of moderation, splitting our focus between two core methodologies: proactive and reactive. Proactive moderation is about setting the stage for positive interactions—being the community gardener who plants seeds of good conversation and weeds out potential problems before they can take root. Reactive moderation, on the other hand, is the emergency response—dealing with inappropriate content after it has been posted. Both are essential, and we will explore the techniques for each in detail.

Finding the right balance between human oversight and technological assistance is a critical theme. We will dissect the ongoing debate between manual and automated moderation, showing how they can work in concert. This leads directly into the burgeoning field of AI-powered tools, which are revolutionizing the speed and scale at which moderation can occur. However, as we will discuss, artificial intelligence is a powerful tool, not a panacea. It comes with its own set of biases and limitations, making the human element more important than ever.

Of course, moderation is not a solo endeavor. We will dedicate significant time to the art and science of building, training, and managing a moderation team. This includes everything from recruiting the right people to providing them with the training and support they need to succeed. A special focus will be given to the psychological toll of the job—a critical issue that is too often overlooked. Moderators are exposed to the worst of the web on a daily basis, and protecting their well-being is paramount to the long-term success of any moderation effort.

The book will also equip you to handle the most challenging aspects of community management. We will provide strategies for dealing with trolls, spammers, and other malicious actors whose goal is not to participate but to disrupt. We will delve into conflict resolution and de-escalation, providing techniques to cool down heated arguments and guide passionate discussions back to a constructive path. You will learn how to manage large-scale incidents and crises, developing a plan for when things go wrong in a very public way.

No guide to moderation would be complete without a thorough examination of the legal and ethical landscape. We will navigate the complex web of laws and regulations that govern online content, including cornerstone legislation like Section 230 of the Communications Decency Act and international standards like the GDPR. Understanding your legal responsibilities and liabilities is not just good practice; it is essential for protecting your platform and your users. Beyond the law, we will grapple with the complex ethics of moderation, exploring the ongoing debate between free expression and safety and the importance of transparency in building community trust.

Finally, we will look toward the future. We will explore the challenges of moderating across different platforms and cultures, the psychology behind why people behave the way they do online, and how to empower your community members to participate in the moderation process themselves. We will cover how to scale your efforts as your community grows and how to measure success, proving the value of your work to stakeholders. The field of online community moderation is constantly evolving, and this book aims to provide you with a durable framework for thinking about and practicing it, no matter what new technologies or social trends emerge.

Our approach throughout will be straightforward and pragmatic. This is not a book of abstract theories but a manual for practitioners. We will state the facts plainly, offer actionable advice, and maintain a neutral perspective on controversial issues. The goal is to provide you with the knowledge and confidence to handle the immense responsibility of managing user-generated content, enabling you to build spaces where people can connect, share, and create in a positive and meaningful way. The work is challenging, often thankless, but utterly essential to the health of our digital world. Let's begin.

CHAPTER ONE: The Foundation of Online Communities

Before one can moderate a community, one must first understand what it truly is. An online community is far more than a piece of software or a collection of user accounts. It is a social ecosystem, a group of people who come together in a digital space to interact, share, and pursue a common interest or goal. A website with user-generated content but no interaction is merely a publication with an audience. A true community requires connection not just between the platform and the user, but between the users themselves. They are defined by the relationships and the shared culture that emerge from these persistent conversations.

At its core, every successful online community possesses a few fundamental components. First, there is a shared purpose, the magnetic force that draws individuals together. This could be a passion for a particular video game, the need for support while navigating a health diagnosis, or a shared professional identity. Second, there are the members, the lifeblood of the community who create content, start conversations, and build relationships. Third is the platform, the virtual space—be it a forum, a social media group, or a dedicated app—that provides the architecture for interaction. Finally, and most crucially, there is the interaction itself, the ongoing exchange that builds the norms and culture unique to that digital tribe.

The concept of digital fellowship is nearly as old as the internet itself. The earliest seeds were planted in the text-heavy environments of the 1970s and 1980s with Bulletin Board Systems (BBS) and Usenet. These were pioneering, if primitive, platforms where users, often connecting via screeching dial-up modems, could post messages and share files on topic-specific "newsgroups" or boards. Participation required a degree of technical skill, which naturally cultivated small, focused communities of academics, researchers, and hobbyists who were passionate about the new frontier of digital communication.

These early systems established many of the foundational principles of online interaction. Usenet, launched in 1980, was a decentralized discussion system with "newsgroups" covering a vast range of topics, from science to recreation. It was a precursor to modern forums, introducing the concept of threaded discussions that allowed for coherent, ongoing conversations. The culture of these early spaces was characterized by a strong sense of shared discovery and self-regulation, as users collaboratively developed norms of behavior, known as "netiquette," to govern their interactions in this new social realm.

The 1990s, with the rise of more accessible internet service providers like AOL, brought online communities to the masses. Forums and chat rooms became mainstream, moving beyond purely technical audiences. Platforms with graphical interfaces lowered the barrier to entry, allowing people to gather around hobbies, favorite TV shows, or musical artists. This era solidified the forum as a dominant model for community, with dedicated spaces for deep, topic-specific discussions that could be archived and searched, creating a lasting repository of collective knowledge.

The dawn of the new millennium marked a significant turning point with the emergence of the first true social networking sites. Platforms like Friendster and MySpace shifted the focus from shared interests to the individual's real-life social network. The community was no longer just about the topic; it was about connecting with friends and showcasing personal identity through customizable profiles. MySpace, in particular, became a cultural phenomenon, reaching a million active users around 2004 and demonstrating the massive commercial and social potential of user-driven online spaces.

This trend culminated in the undisputed dominance of platforms like Facebook, which began in 2004. These mega-platforms fundamentally altered the landscape by consolidating various types of communities under one digital roof. Instead of visiting a dozen different forums for a dozen different interests, users could join groups, follow pages, and interact with brands all within a single, algorithmically-curated feed. This centralization brought convenience and scale but also introduced new moderation challenges as the lines between distinct communities began to blur.

The modern landscape is a hybrid of this history, a fragmented and diverse ecosystem. While massive social networks remain dominant, there has been a significant return to niche platforms. Services like Reddit, Discord, and Slack have enabled the creation of highly specialized and interactive communities, blending the topic-focus of old-school forums with the real-time communication of chat rooms. At the same time, the creator economy has spawned a new type of community, with influencers, writers, and artists building dedicated followings on platforms like Patreon and Substack, where the community forms around the personality and their work.

To effectively manage a community, it is essential to recognize what kind of digital tribe you are dealing with. Though the lines can blur, most online communities can be categorized by their primary purpose. Understanding this purpose is the first step in tailoring a moderation strategy that fits the members' expectations and goals. Each type has a different social dynamic, different user needs, and, consequently, different moderation requirements.

Perhaps the most common type is the **Community of Interest**. These are groups formed around a shared hobby, passion, or fandom. Whether it's a forum for classic car restoration, a subreddit for a popular television series, or a Facebook group for urban gardeners, the binding agent is a mutual love for a specific topic. Engagement is often driven by enthusiasm and the desire to share knowledge, news, and creations with like-minded peers.

Then there are **Communities of Practice**. These are professional networks where members share insights, solve problems, and advance their skills in a particular field. Examples include developer forums where programmers debug code together, LinkedIn groups for marketing professionals, or private Slack channels for entrepreneurs. In these spaces, the value lies in knowledge sharing, mentorship, and networking for career advancement.

Support Communities serve a vital human need, offering a space for individuals navigating similar life challenges. These can be forums for patients with a specific medical condition, groups for new parents, or communities for people dealing with grief. The core purpose is to provide emotional support, empathy, and practical advice in a safe and non-judgmental environment where members can connect over shared lived experiences.

While the internet transcends geography, **Communities of Place** are explicitly tied to a physical location. Neighborhood Facebook groups, city-specific subreddits, and platforms like Nextdoor connect people who live in the same area. These communities focus on local news, events, recommendations for services, and discussions about civic issues. They blend online interaction with real-world relevance, creating a digital parallel to a town square.

Many businesses cultivate **Brand Communities** to foster loyalty and engage directly with their customers. These can range from official support forums where users can troubleshoot product issues to fan groups where enthusiasts share their passion for a company's products. These spaces are valuable for gathering customer feedback, providing support, and building an emotional connection that turns customers into advocates.

Finally, **Gaming Communities** represent a massive and highly engaged segment of the online world. From guilds in massively multiplayer online games (MMOs) to Discord servers for fans of a particular streamer, these communities are built around shared play. They are often characterized by intense social interaction, collaborative problem-solving, and the formation of strong, lasting friendships forged through shared virtual experiences.

Understanding the different types of communities is only half the picture. We must also understand the fundamental human motivations that drive people to join and participate in the first place. These psychological drivers are universal, and tapping into them is key to fostering a vibrant and self-sustaining community. At the most basic level, people are seeking connection and a sense of belonging.

One of the most powerful motivators is the simple, profound human need to belong. Maslow's hierarchy of needs identifies social connection as a vital component of emotional well-being. Online communities provide a space for individuals to find "their people," connecting with others who share their interests, values, or life experiences, which can be particularly reassuring for those with niche hobbies or who feel isolated in their offline lives.

Beyond simple belonging, people join communities to engage in **information exchange**. Whether seeking advice on a technical problem, learning a new skill, or simply staying up-to-date on a topic of interest, communities act as powerful reservoirs of collective knowledge. New members can learn from veterans, and experts can refine their understanding by teaching others. This dynamic creates a mutually beneficial ecosystem of learning and growth.

Participation is also a form of **identity validation and self-expression**. Online communities offer a stage where individuals can express their thoughts and opinions and receive feedback from their peers. This interaction helps to reinforce one's sense of self and expertise. Achieving recognition within a group, whether through upvotes, special titles, or simply being known as a helpful member, is a powerful form of social validation that encourages continued engagement.

Of course, many join for **entertainment and recreation**. Communities can be a source of immense fun, a place to share jokes, participate in games and contests, and enjoy lighthearted conversations. This is particularly true for fandom and gaming communities, where the shared enjoyment of a piece of media or a virtual world is the primary draw. The community itself becomes an extension of the entertainment experience.

Finally, some communities are built around **shared goals and collective action**. These "communities of action" are formed to organize events, raise money for a cause, or advocate for political change. Members are motivated by the desire to make a tangible impact and achieve something together that they could not accomplish alone. This shared purpose can create incredibly strong bonds and a powerful sense of efficacy.

Just like any living system, an online community evolves. It goes through a predictable lifecycle, and understanding these stages helps a moderator anticipate challenges and adapt their strategy accordingly. The needs of a community in its infancy are vastly different from those of a large, mature one. Recognizing where your community is in its journey is critical for effective management.

The first stage is **Inception**. This is the very beginning, when the community is just an idea or a newly launched platform. The initial focus is on attracting the first core members. Engagement is low and often needs to be kickstarted by the community manager, who might personally invite initial users, initiate discussions, and create foundational content. This phase is characterized by high effort for seemingly low returns, but it's essential for setting the cultural tone.

Next comes the **Establishment** phase. At this point, the community has started to gain some traction. New members are joining more organically, and user-generated content is beginning to flow without constant prompting. A sense of community starts to form as norms develop and early members become regulars. This is typically when the first real moderation challenges appear, such as interpersonal conflicts or off-topic posts, requiring the formalization of rules and guidelines.

If the community continues to thrive, it enters the **Maturity** stage. Membership growth may slow to a more stable rate, but engagement from existing members is high. The community has a well-defined culture, established traditions, and often, a core group of veteran members or "super users" who help guide newcomers and contribute significantly to the content. The community is largely self-sustaining at this point, with the moderator's role shifting from content generation to facilitation and high-level oversight.

The final potential stage is one of **Division or Decline**. No community lasts forever. This stage, sometimes called Mitosis, can occur when a mature community becomes so large that it splinters into smaller, more specialized sub-groups. Alternatively, it can enter a period of decline as members lose interest, the platform becomes technologically outdated, or the central topic of interest fades in relevance. A proactive moderator may manage this by facilitating the creation of subgroups or planning a graceful migration to a new platform.

Underpinning the entire community lifecycle is an invisible but crucial currency: **social capital**. In this context, social capital refers to the value—the resources, trust, and mutual support—that members derive from their network of relationships within the community. It is the collective goodwill and collaborative spirit that makes a group of individuals more than the sum of its parts. A community rich in social capital is resilient, helpful, and welcoming.

Social capital comes in several forms. Bonding social capital refers to the strong ties between similar people within a group, like the close friendships that form in a tight-knit support community. Bridging social capital, on the other hand, involves weaker ties between more diverse groups, such as the connections made between professionals from different industries in a networking community. Both are essential for a healthy ecosystem.

Trust is the bedrock upon which social capital is built. In an online environment, trust is cultivated through consistent, positive interactions. It grows when members see others being helpful, when they share personal experiences and receive supportive responses, and when they observe that the rules are enforced fairly for everyone. Every helpful answer, every welcoming comment, and every constructive debate is a small deposit into the community's bank of social capital.

Reputation systems are a common way that platforms attempt to formalize and visualize social capital. Features like likes, upvotes, follower counts, member ratings, and special badges all serve as signals of a user's standing and trustworthiness within the community. These systems provide a shortcut for members to quickly assess who is a knowledgeable expert, a helpful contributor, or a long-standing member of the group.

Malicious behavior, such as trolling, spam, and harassment, is a direct attack on this trust. These actions erode social capital by making members feel unsafe, devaluing conversations, and creating a hostile environment. This is why moderation is not simply about cleaning up messes; it is the primary mechanism for protecting and nurturing the social capital that makes the community a valuable place to be. By removing bad actors, moderators preserve the integrity of the space for everyone else.

Finally, the very architecture of a community's platform plays a foundational role in shaping user behavior. The design choices, features, and limitations of the software itself create a framework that encourages certain types of interactions while discouraging others. A platform designed for long-form, threaded discussions, like a traditional forum, will foster a different kind of community than a platform built for rapid-fire, real-time chat, like Discord.

Consider the difference between an anonymous and a real-name platform. A community that requires users to use their real identities, like LinkedIn or a neighborhood group on Facebook, often sees more civil behavior because users' offline reputations are at stake. Conversely, a platform that allows for anonymity or pseudonymity, like Reddit or 4chan, may foster freer expression but can also lower the barrier for antisocial behavior, making moderation more complex.

Features like content sorting algorithms also have a profound impact. A community platform that sorts content chronologically will have a very different feel from one that uses an algorithm to prioritize posts based on engagement metrics like likes or comments. An algorithmic feed can increase engagement with popular content but may also create filter bubbles or amplify outrage and controversy for the sake of clicks, posing a unique moderation challenge.

Even the smallest design elements can influence behavior. The presence or absence of a downvote button, the character limit on posts, the ease with which users can report content, and the visibility of moderation actions all send subtle signals to the community about what is valued and expected. A skilled moderator understands that they are not just managing people; they are operating within a system whose design is constantly nudging users in certain directions. Understanding these foundational elements—what a community is, its history, its types, its motivations, its lifecycle, and the social and technical structures that support it—is the essential first step on the path to effective moderation.

CHAPTER TWO: The Role and Responsibilities of a Community Moderator

If an online community is a digital city, as we have suggested, then the moderator is not a single person but a committee of municipal workers rolled into one. They are simultaneously the friendly tour guide welcoming newcomers, the diligent janitor sweeping away spam, the referee ensuring fair play, the diplomat mediating disputes, and the lifeguard watching for signs of trouble. It is a multifaceted, deeply human role that is often misunderstood. The pervasive stereotype is that of a power-hungry volunteer on a mission to censor dissent. The reality is that effective moderation is a subtle craft requiring a delicate balance of authority, empathy, and strategic invisibility.

At its core, the moderator's purpose is to act as a guardian of the community's health and culture. Their primary function is to cultivate and protect a safe, respectful, and engaging environment where members feel comfortable participating. This is not about controlling the conversation, but about ensuring a conversation can happen in the first place. Without this foundational layer of safety and order, communities can quickly descend into a chaotic state where the loudest, most aggressive voices drown out all others, driving away the thoughtful members who make the community valuable.

The responsibilities of a moderator can be broadly divided into two categories: proactive and reactive. While we will explore these methodologies in greater detail in later chapters, it is essential to understand them as the two primary pillars of the moderator's work. Proactive work is about building and nurturing, while reactive work is about protecting and repairing. A great moderator spends far more time on the former, as successful proactive efforts naturally reduce the need for reactive interventions.

The most visible responsibility is, of course, the enforcement of community guidelines. Moderators are tasked with reviewing user-generated content—posts, comments, images, videos—to ensure it complies with the established rules. This involves removing content that violates policies on hate speech, harassment, spam, or other prohibited behaviors. However, this is not a purely mechanical task. It requires careful judgment to interpret the rules in context, understand nuance and intent, and apply them consistently and fairly to all members, regardless of their status or popularity within the community.

Beyond simply removing bad content, a moderator is also a facilitator of good conversation. This is a key proactive responsibility. They can spark engagement by posing interesting questions, starting new discussions, and highlighting valuable contributions from other members. In a new or quiet community, the moderator may need to be the primary conversationalist, keeping the space active and making it feel lived-in until user-led engagement reaches a self-sustaining level. They act as the host of the party, ensuring everyone feels welcome and has a chance to speak.

A crucial, though often behind-the-scenes, part of the job is conflict resolution. When disagreements between members escalate into personal attacks or flame wars, the moderator must step in. This rarely involves taking a side in the argument itself. Instead, the moderator's role is to de-escalate the tension, remind the participants of the community's behavioral standards, and guide the conversation back to a constructive path. It requires a calm demeanor and the ability to act as a neutral third party focused on the health of the overall discussion, not the specifics of the dispute.

Moderators also serve as the frontline of member support. They are the most visible representatives of the platform or brand, making them the first point of contact for users with questions, concerns, or technical problems. This can range from answering simple questions about how to use a platform feature to helping a distressed user who is being harassed. This aspect of the role requires a service-oriented mindset and a great deal of patience, as they are often dealing with people who are confused, frustrated, or upset.

Another vital function is acting as the bridge between the community and the platform's owners or administrators. Moderators have their finger on the pulse of the community. They understand the members' collective mood, their frustrations, and their desires. A key responsibility is to gather this feedback and communicate it to the people who make strategic decisions about the community's future. This ensures that the platform evolves in a way that serves the needs of its users, not just the assumptions of its creators.

To successfully juggle these varied responsibilities, an individual must possess a unique combination of skills and personal qualities. These are not traits one is necessarily born with; they are muscles that can be developed through training and experience. The first and most important of these is unimpeachable impartiality. A moderator must be able to enforce the rules fairly and consistently, without personal bias. They cannot play favorites or let their personal feelings about a topic or a member influence their decisions. The community must trust that the rules apply equally to everyone.

Exceptional communication skills are non-negotiable. Since nearly all of a moderator's work is conducted through text, the ability to write with clarity, precision, and empathy is paramount. They must be able to explain their actions clearly, de-escalate tense situations with carefully chosen words, and communicate policies without sounding robotic or authoritarian. Misunderstandings are rife in text-based communication, and a skilled moderator knows how to avoid them and clear them up when they happen.

Patience and a thick skin are indispensable. Moderators are the designated recipients of community frustration. They will be criticized, insulted, and accused of bias, often for simply doing their job. The ability to remain calm under pressure, absorb criticism without taking it personally, and respond to anger with professionalism is crucial for long-term survival in the role. This emotional resilience is one of the most challenging, yet essential, aspects of the job.

Sound judgment is the bedrock of every moderation decision. Many situations a moderator faces will not be black and white. They will fall into gray areas where the rules are open to interpretation. In these moments, a moderator must rely on critical thinking and a deep understanding of the community's culture and values to make a defensible decision. They have to weigh the importance of free expression against the need for safety and civility, often in a matter of minutes.

A deep, authentic understanding of the community itself is also vital. The best moderators are often homegrown—long-standing members who have a natural feel for the group's specific social norms, inside jokes, and history. This allows them to moderate with a human touch, making decisions that are not just technically correct according to the rules, but culturally appropriate for that specific community. This intrinsic knowledge is difficult to replicate and is a key differentiator between an effective moderator and a blunt instrument of enforcement.

Finally, discretion and professionalism are key. Moderators are often privy to sensitive information, from user data and private reports of abuse to internal discussions about future platform changes. They must be trusted to handle this information with confidentiality. Their public-facing communication must always be professional, even when dealing with difficult users, as they are acting as a representative of the community and its leadership.

While the title is singular, the moderator role can take different forms depending on the context. The most common distinction is between volunteer and professional moderators. Volunteer moderators are typically passionate members of the community who dedicate their free time to helping manage the space. They are motivated by a love for the community and a desire to maintain its quality. Many of the largest platforms on the internet, such as Reddit and Discord, are built on the backs of millions of hours of unpaid volunteer labor.

Professional moderators, on the other hand, are paid employees. They may work directly for a large social media company, a brand that hosts its own customer community, or a third-party moderation service provider. For them, moderation is a full-time job with set hours, performance metrics, and a formal command structure. While they may not always have the same deep-seated passion as a volunteer, they bring a level of professional detachment and accountability that is essential for large-scale operations.

The line can often blur between a moderator and a Community Manager. While the terms are sometimes used interchangeably, they generally represent two distinct, though overlapping, functions. A moderator's role is primarily focused on the day-to-day enforcement of rules and management of content within the community. It is largely a reactive and tactical role, dealing with issues as they arise.

A Community Manager, by contrast, typically operates at a more strategic level. While they may perform moderation tasks, their primary responsibilities include developing the overall community strategy, planning engagement campaigns, analyzing community health metrics, and representing the community's interests at a business level. Put simply, the moderator tends the garden day-to-day, while the community manager is the landscape architect planning the garden's future. In smaller communities, one person often wears both hats.

Regardless of the specific title or pay structure, the person in this role must be a master of context-switching, embodying several archetypes in the course of a single day. They are the welcoming **Host**, greeting new members and making them feel comfortable. They are the **Librarian**, organizing information, tagging threads, and ensuring valuable content is easy to find. They are the **Event Planner**, organizing contests, Q&A sessions, or other activities to spur engagement.

More critically, they are the **Referee**, watching the flow of conversation and blowing the whistle when a foul is committed.

They must do this fairly, calling fouls on both teams without bias. They are the **Diplomat**, stepping between feuding parties to mediate a truce and prevent a small disagreement from becoming a community-wide brawl. And, when all else fails, they are the **Security Guard**, ejecting individuals who are intent on causing harm and disrupting the safety of the space for everyone else.

Understanding this complex and demanding set of responsibilities is the first step toward appreciating the true value of a good moderator. They are not merely janitors or censors. They are cultivators of conversation, protectors of community culture, and the essential human element that allows a group of strangers to come together and create something valuable online. Their work, when done well, is often invisible, but its absence is immediately and painfully obvious.

CHAPTER THREE: Establishing Clear Community Guidelines and Policies

If the moderator is the guardian of the community, then the community guidelines are their charter and their most essential tool. They are the foundational legal code of your digital society, the constitution upon which all subsequent actions are based. A community without clear, written rules is not a utopia of free expression; it is a ticking time bomb of misunderstandings, conflict, and chaos. When disputes arise, as they inevitably will, having a public set of standards to point to transforms a moderator's decision from a personal judgment into an impartial application of established policy. This single document is the bedrock of fairness and predictability.

The primary purpose of community guidelines is to set expectations. They explicitly inform every member, from the day-one newcomer to the seasoned veteran, what constitutes acceptable and unacceptable behavior. This simple act of clarification preemptively solves a vast number of potential problems. People cannot be expected to follow rules they do not know exist. By laying out the standards of conduct upfront, you provide a framework that empowers the vast majority of well-intentioned users to participate constructively and avoid inadvertently causing friction.

Furthermore, these guidelines serve as a crucial shield for both the moderators and the platform itself. For moderators, they are a source of authority and a defense against accusations of bias. An action is no longer "a decision I made because I didn't like your post," but rather, "an action I took because your post violated Guideline 3b." For the platform, particularly for businesses, well-defined and consistently enforced guidelines are a vital component in mitigating legal risk and demonstrating a commitment to user safety.

It is critical to distinguish between community guidelines and a Terms of Service (ToS) or End-User License Agreement (EULA). Think of it this way: the Terms of Service is the dense, legally-binding contract written by lawyers for the company's protection. It covers complex topics like intellectual property rights, liability, and jurisdiction. The community guidelines, on the other hand, are the user-friendly social contract written by community managers for the community's health. They are meant to be read, understood, and followed by everyday users, translating the legalese of the ToS into practical, behavioral do's and don'ts.

The most effective guidelines are built on a foundation of core principles. First and foremost is **Clarity**. The language used must be simple, direct, and unambiguous. Avoid corporate jargon, technical slang, or convoluted legalistic phrasing. The goal is to be understood by the widest possible audience, including users who may not be native speakers of the language. A good test is to ask whether a brand-new member could read the rules once and have a solid grasp of how to behave. If it requires a law degree to interpret, it has failed.

Brevity is clarity's close cousin. In an age of diminishing attention spans, a twenty-page document of rules is a document that will not be read. Guidelines should be as concise as possible without sacrificing essential detail. Use bullet points, clear headings, and bold text to make the document scannable. A user should be able to find the relevant rule quickly. If your guidelines are becoming unwieldy, consider using a main page with the core rules and linking out to more detailed explanations for specific policies, like those on self-promotion or content formatting.

The rules must also be **Comprehensive**. While brevity is a virtue, the guidelines must be thorough enough to cover the most common and predictable issues that arise in your community. A good starting point is to think about the types of negative behavior common to the internet—personal attacks, spam, hate speech, illegal content—and address them head-on. It is far better to have a rule you rarely use than to be caught without a rule when a new and disruptive behavior emerges.

Accessibility is paramount. The most brilliantly written guidelines are useless if no one can find them. They should be prominently linked in highly visible locations. This includes the community's main navigation, the registration page for new users, and pinned posts in the most active forums or channels. Some platforms even require new users to explicitly check a box stating they have read and agreed to the guidelines before they are allowed to post for the first time, a simple step that reinforces their importance from the outset.

Finally, and most critically, guidelines must be **Enforceable**. Do not create rules that you do not have the resources, technical capability, or willpower to enforce. An unenforced rule is worse than no rule at all; it undermines the credibility of all the other rules and signals to the community that the standards are merely suggestions. If you declare a zero-tolerance policy for a certain behavior, you must be prepared to enforce it every time, or the policy becomes meaningless.

While every community is unique, a robust set of guidelines typically includes several key components. It is often wise to begin with a **Preamble or Mission Statement**. This is a brief, positive introduction that sets the tone. Instead of starting with a list of prohibitions, begin by explaining what the community is *for*. What is its purpose? What kind of environment are you trying to create? This frames the rules not as arbitrary restrictions, but as necessary measures to achieve a shared, positive goal. For example, "Welcome to our community of gardeners! This is a place to share tips, celebrate successes, and help each other grow. To keep this a friendly and productive space, we ask that you follow these guidelines."

Following the preamble, you should outline the core behavioral rules. These are the fundamental "Don'ts" that form the backbone of your moderation policy. The most universal and important rule is usually some variation of **"Be Respectful"** or **"No Personal Attacks."** This is where you prohibit insults, ad hominem arguments, harassment, and bullying. It is helpful to provide brief examples. For instance, "Debate the idea, not the person. It is fine to say 'I disagree with your point for these reasons,' but not 'You're an idiot for thinking that.'"

Directly related to this is a policy against **Hate Speech and Discrimination**. This rule should explicitly forbid any content that promotes discrimination, disparages, or harasses individuals or groups based on characteristics like race, ethnicity, religion, gender identity, sexual orientation, age, disability, or national origin. This is a non-negotiable component for creating a safe and inclusive environment.

Nearly every community needs a rule against **Illegal Content and Activities**. This serves as a catch-all to prohibit discussions or distributions of illegal materials, such as pirated software or copyrighted content, as well as forbidding threats of violence, the sharing of private information without consent (doxxing), and any content that exploits or endangers minors. While these are often covered in the Terms of Service, repeating them in the guidelines in plain language is essential.

Spam is the eternal scourge of the internet, making a clear **"No Spam"** rule indispensable. This is also where you should define your policy on **Self-Promotion**. A blanket ban is not always the best approach. A more nuanced policy might allow members to share their own work in a specific thread or on a certain day of the week, provided they are also active and contributing members of the community in other ways. This allows you to differentiate between a hit-and-run spammer and a valued community member sharing a relevant project.

Rules about **Staying On-Topic** are crucial for communities of interest or practice. If your forum is dedicated to classic car restoration, discussions about politics or sports can derail conversations and frustrate members who are there for the core subject matter. This rule allows moderators to gently redirect or remove off-topic content to maintain the community's focus and purpose.

Depending on the nature of your community, you may need a variety of **Content-Specific Rules**. For a visual community, this might include rules about not posting Not Safe For Work (NSFW) or graphic content. For a fan community discussing a television series, a clear and strict policy on how to handle and tag spoilers is essential to prevent ruining the experience for others. For a support community, you might need a rule against giving unqualified medical or legal advice.

It is also wise to include a section on **Account and Profile Rules**. This is where you can prohibit impersonation of other users, the creation of multiple accounts to evade a ban or manipulate voting, and the use of offensive usernames or avatars. These rules help maintain the integrity of user identities within the community.

After outlining the "Don'ts," it is highly effective to include a section of "Do's," framed as **Community Best Practices**. This shifts the tone from prohibitive to encouraging. Here, you can prompt users to use descriptive titles for their posts, to search for existing topics before starting a new one, to welcome newcomers, and to contribute to a constructive and friendly atmosphere. This helps to codify the positive aspects of your desired community culture.

Crucially, your guidelines must explain the **Consequences of Violating the Rules**. Transparency in enforcement is key to building trust. This section should outline the typical progression of moderation actions, often called an "escalation ladder." This might start with a friendly public reminder or a private warning for a minor first offense, followed by content removal, a temporary suspension (or "timeout"), and ultimately, a permanent ban for repeated or severe violations. Be sure to state that the severity of the action will match the severity of the violation; for example, posting illegal content would result in an immediate permanent ban, skipping the warning steps.

This section should also detail the **Appeals Process**. No moderator is infallible, and providing a clear path for users to appeal a decision shows a commitment to fairness. This process need not be complicated. It could be as simple as providing a specific email address or a private contact form where users can state their case. The appeal should be reviewed, if possible, by a different moderator or a community manager to ensure an unbiased second look.

When you sit down to write your guidelines, it can be tempting to simply copy and paste a set from a similar community. While looking at other communities for inspiration is a great starting point, your guidelines must be tailored to the specific context, culture, and purpose of your own community. A set of rules designed for a fast-paced gaming Discord server will be a poor fit for a medical support forum for seniors.

Involving the community in the creation or revision of guidelines can be a powerful way to increase buy-in, particularly in an established community. You could post a draft and ask for feedback, allowing members to voice concerns or suggest clarifications. This collaborative process can make users feel a sense of ownership over their community and its standards, turning them into active allies in upholding the rules.

Once your guidelines are written, they must be treated as a living document. Online culture and behavior are constantly evolving, and new challenges will inevitably arise that your initial rules did not anticipate. A new type of spam might emerge, or a new social media trend might start causing disruptions. It is good practice to schedule a formal review of the guidelines on a regular basis, perhaps every six or twelve months, to ensure they are still relevant and effective.

When you do make changes to the guidelines, it is vital to communicate these changes clearly and proactively to the community. Announce the updates in a prominent post, explain the reasoning behind the changes, and give members an opportunity to ask questions. Suddenly enforcing a new rule that members were not aware of is a sure way to create resentment and distrust. Transparency in the evolution of the rules is just as important as transparency in their enforcement. Your guidelines are the single most important document you will create in the service of your community. They are a declaration of your values, a manual for your members, and a toolkit for your moderators. Investing the time and thought to make them clear, fair, and comprehensive is the first, and most important, step in building a thriving and resilient online space.

CHAPTER FOUR: Proactive Moderation: Setting the Tone for Positive Engagement

Imagine two community spaces. The first is a room where the host only appears when a fight breaks out, to throw the offenders onto the street and then disappear again. The second is a lively gathering where the host greets you at the door, introduces you to others, starts interesting conversations, and subtly keeps an eye on things, ensuring the atmosphere remains friendly and welcoming. While both hosts are technically moderating the space, the experience for guests is worlds apart. The first is practicing purely reactive moderation; the second has mastered the art of proactive moderation.

Proactive moderation is the ongoing, often subtle, work of creating an environment where positive behavior is the norm and negative behavior feels out of place. It is the gardening to reactive moderation's firefighting. While you must be prepared to put out fires, a well-tended garden with healthy soil and properly spaced plants is far less likely to have widespread blazes in the first place. The goal of a proactive strategy is not to prevent every single rule violation, but to build a resilient community culture that naturally encourages constructive participation and marginalizes disruptive conduct. This is the difference between being a janitor and being an architect.

The journey for any member begins with their first impression, and this is where proactive work starts. The onboarding process is your first and best chance to set the tone. A new user arriving in a silent, empty community is likely to leave immediately. Conversely, a user who is greeted warmly and guided on how to participate is far more likely to stick around and become a contributing member. A simple, automated welcome message or email is a good baseline, but it lacks the personal touch that builds real connection.

A far more effective technique is to create a dedicated space for introductions. A pinned "Introduce Yourself" or "Welcome New Members!" thread is a classic for a reason. It provides a low-stakes first step for participation. The moderator's job is to be the first to respond to these new introductions. A simple "Welcome, [Username]! Glad to have you here. I see you're interested in [Topic]. You might want to check out this discussion over here..." does two things: it provides immediate positive reinforcement and it actively directs the new member toward relevant content, helping them integrate more quickly.

This initial welcome is also the perfect opportunity to gently reinforce the community's standards. Instead of hitting them over the head with a list of rules, you can frame it positively. For instance, a welcome email might include a line like, "To help you get started, you can find our community guidelines here. They're our shared agreement for keeping this a friendly and respectful place for everyone." This presents the rules not as a list of punishments, but as a tool for collective well-being, a concept introduced in the previous chapter.

Beyond formal welcomes, moderators must lead by example in every interaction. Community members, especially new ones, look to the moderators and administrators to understand the unwritten rules and the acceptable tone of the space. Every post a moderator makes is a lesson in cultural norms. If a moderator is sarcastic, dismissive, or overly aggressive, it signals that this behavior is acceptable for everyone. If they are helpful, patient, and respectful—even when dealing with difficult users—it sets a powerful precedent.

This modeling of behavior is particularly crucial when handling disagreements. A moderator should actively demonstrate how to disagree constructively. Instead of ignoring a debate or letting it fester, a proactive moderator might jump in with a comment that elevates the discourse. Something as simple as, "These are both really interesting points of view. @UserA, can you expand on why you think X? @UserB, have you considered this angle?" can reframe a potential argument into a productive discussion and show others how to engage with differing opinions respectfully.

Of course, a community can't run on greetings and good vibes alone. It needs content and conversation. In a new or slow-moving community, the moderator must often take on the role of conversation-starter. This is the practice of "content seeding"— strategically posting content and questions designed to elicit responses and get members talking to each other. The key is to avoid closed-ended questions that can be answered with a simple "yes" or "no" and instead favor open-ended prompts. "What's the biggest challenge you're facing with X this week?" will generate far more discussion than "Are you having challenges with X?"

Creating a predictable rhythm for content can also be highly effective. Establishing recurring weekly threads builds a sense of routine and gives members a reason to check in regularly. "Tech Tuesday," "Showcase Saturday," or "Weekly Goals Monday" all create consistent, low-effort opportunities for engagement. The moderator's initial job is to launch these threads consistently and participate in them enthusiastically until they gain enough momentum to become self-sustaining user-led traditions.

As the community grows and user-generated content begins to flow, the proactive moderator's role shifts from content creator to content curator. Their job is now to highlight and reward the kind of contributions they want to see more of. Positive reinforcement is a far more powerful tool for shaping behavior than negative punishment. When you see a member post a particularly insightful comment, a helpful tutorial, or a welcoming reply to a newcomer, amplify it.

This amplification can take many forms. It can be as simple as a public reply: "This is an incredibly helpful answer, thank you for taking the time to write it up!" It could involve using platform features to "pin" or "feature" an excellent post so it stays at the top of the feed for longer. Some platforms allow for the creation of a "Best Of" section or a weekly "Community Roundup" newsletter, providing a formal mechanism for showcasing high-quality contributions and recognizing the members who created them.

Formalizing this recognition through gamification and reputation systems can be even more effective. Features like special user flairs ("Community Expert," "Top Contributor"), unique badges, or a points system that unlocks new abilities all serve as tangible rewards for positive participation. These systems tap into the fundamental human desires for status and recognition, creating a virtuous cycle where members are motivated to contribute constructively in order to build their reputation within the group. This is the practical application of building the social capital we discussed in Chapter One.

The very structure of the community space is another powerful proactive tool. Thoughtful organization can guide user behavior and prevent common problems before they occur. A sprawling, disorganized forum with a single "General Discussion" category is an invitation for chaos. A well-structured community with clear, logically-named channels or sub-forums helps users post their content in the right place and find the information they need without getting frustrated. For example, creating a dedicated "Off-Topic" or "Water Cooler" channel provides a sanctioned outlet for conversations that don't fit elsewhere, preventing them from derailing more focused discussions.

The strategic use of pinned posts and Frequently Asked Questions (FAQ) documents is another cornerstone of proactive structural moderation. By identifying the most common questions newcomers ask and providing clear, comprehensive answers in a highly visible, permanently-affixed post, you can dramatically reduce the number of repetitive queries. This not only saves moderators' time but also empowers new users to find answers for themselves, giving them a sense of competence and making the community appear well-organized and helpful from the moment they arrive.

Some platforms offer even more granular tools for shaping behavior. Post templates, for instance, can be used in support forums or bug-reporting sections to prompt users to provide all the necessary information upfront. A template might include fields for "Device," "Operating System," and "Steps to Reproduce the Issue." This structuring ensures that moderators and other community members have the information they need to help, preventing the frustrating and time-consuming back-and-forth of "Have you tried turning it off and on again?"

More subtle interventions can also nudge the community in the right direction. If a discussion is beginning to drift into unproductive territory, a proactive moderator can gently redirect it without needing to issue a formal warning. A comment like, "This is getting a bit off-topic for this particular thread. If you'd like to discuss [new topic], feel free to start a new discussion in the [Off-Topic section]!" validates the members' interest while protecting the integrity of the original conversation.

Automated tools can also play a proactive role. Word filters, for example, can be configured to automatically block or flag posts containing racial slurs or other egregious violations. This acts as a first line of defense, preventing the most toxic content from ever becoming visible to the wider community. However, these tools must be used with care. Overly aggressive filters can lead to false positives, censoring benign conversations and frustrating users whose posts are unfairly flagged. They are a supplement to, not a replacement for, human judgment.

Ultimately, all of these proactive techniques work together to build a strong, positive community culture. When a space is consistently well-managed, welcoming, and focused on constructive conversation, it creates a powerful sense of social proof. Newcomers see how existing members behave and adjust their own behavior to match the established norms. In a healthy community, the members themselves become an extension of the moderation team. They will welcome new users, answer questions, and report or flag content that violates the spirit of the community, creating a kind of cultural immune system. This reduces the burden on the formal moderation team and makes the entire system more scalable and resilient. Proactive moderation is a continuous investment in the social fabric of your community, and it pays dividends every single day.

CHAPTER FIVE: Reactive Moderation: Responding to Inappropriate Content

No matter how carefully a garden is tended, weeds will inevitably appear. Despite the most thoughtful proactive strategies, a community of any significant size will eventually produce content that violates its guidelines. This is not a sign of failure; it is a simple reality of managing spaces populated by human beings. When a rule is broken, the moderator must shift from the role of architect and host to that of an emergency responder. This is the domain of reactive moderation: the process of identifying, evaluating, and acting upon inappropriate content after it has been posted. It is the necessary, often challenging, work of enforcing the standards that keep the community safe and functional.

While proactive moderation builds a strong cultural immune system, reactive moderation is the targeted medicine administered when that system is breached. The goal is to address violations swiftly, fairly, and consistently, thereby minimizing their negative impact on the broader community. Effective reactive moderation reinforces the integrity of the guidelines, demonstrating to all members that the rules are not merely suggestions but are actively upheld. This process, when handled well, builds trust; when handled poorly, it can quickly erode it, creating an environment of perceived bias and resentment.

The primary engine of reactive moderation is the user reporting system. It is the community's alarm bell, a mechanism that empowers members to flag content they believe violates the rules. This is a critical partnership. A moderation team, no matter its size, cannot be expected to read every single post and comment in real-time. By providing a clear, simple, and accessible "Report" button on all user-generated content, you deputize the entire community, creating millions of extra eyes that can help spot trouble. The design of this feature is crucial; it should be easy to find and straightforward to use, ideally allowing the user to select the specific rule they believe has been violated.

Once a user submits a report, the content enters what is known as the moderation queue. This is the moderator's digital workstation, a centralized dashboard that collects all flagged items for review. The queue is where the process of triage begins. In a busy community, this queue can fill up rapidly, and not all reports carry the same weight or urgency. A moderator must learn to quickly scan the queue and prioritize their attention. An off-topic comment is a low-priority issue; a credible threat of violence or the posting of illegal content is a five-alarm fire that requires immediate attention, dropping everything else.

This triage process involves a rapid initial assessment of severity. Is the content potentially illegal? Does it pose a direct threat to a user's safety? Is it hate speech targeting a protected group? These types of violations must always be moved to the top of the list. Next in priority are issues that directly harm the user experience, such as major spam attacks, severe harassment, or the posting of graphic content in a general-access area. Lower-priority items include minor rule infractions like duplicate posts, mild off-topic discussions, or formatting errors. This prioritization ensures that the most damaging content is removed with the greatest speed.

After identifying a high-priority item, the next step is a brief but crucial investigation. Acting on a report without understanding its context is a recipe for error. A single comment, viewed in isolation, may seem abusive, but when read within the flow of the conversation, it might be revealed as obvious sarcasm between two friends. The moderator must become a quick and efficient digital detective, piecing together the necessary context to make an informed decision. This means looking at the immediate conversational thread, not just the reported post itself.

The investigation might also involve a quick review of the reporting user's history as well as the history of the user who was reported. Is the reported user a long-standing member in good standing who made a one-time mistake, or do they have a documented history of pushing boundaries and causing trouble? Is the reporting user someone who frequently files frivolous reports against people they disagree with? This background information doesn't change whether a rule was broken, but it can provide valuable context that informs which moderation action is most appropriate.

Once the investigation is complete and a rule violation has been confirmed, the moderator must choose the appropriate action from their toolkit. This toolkit can be thought of as an escalation ladder, with responses ranging from a very light touch to the ultimate sanction of a permanent ban. The principle of proportionality is key; the severity of the action should always match the severity of the offense. Over-moderating minor issues can feel draconian and alienate users, while under-moderating serious offenses makes the space feel unsafe.

For the most minor infractions, sometimes the best response is to do nothing at all. If a comment is slightly off-topic but the conversation has already moved on, taking a visible moderation action might be more disruptive than simply letting it fade. In other cases, a very gentle public nudge, such as moving a thread to a more appropriate sub-forum, is sufficient. This action corrects the issue without punishing the user, subtly educating them on the community's structure.

The most common action is **Content Removal**. This simply involves deleting the offending post or comment. Platforms often distinguish between a "soft delete," which hides the content from public view but keeps it visible to moderators and administrators for record-keeping, and a "hard delete," which permanently purges it from the database. The soft delete is almost always preferable, as it preserves evidence should the user appeal the decision or if a pattern of behavior needs to be reviewed later.

In some rare instances, **Editing a User's Content** may be appropriate, but this power should be wielded with extreme caution. Editing can be useful for removing a small piece of problematic content—like personal information or a single slur— from an otherwise valuable post. However, it can also be seen as putting words in a user's mouth. If an edit is performed, it must be accompanied by a clear, public note indicating that the post was edited by a moderator and for what reason (e.g., "[Edited by Mod to remove personal phone number]").

Following a content removal, the next step is often a **Warning**. Warnings serve to educate the user, informing them that they have violated a rule and giving them an opportunity to correct their behavior. These are best delivered privately, via a direct message or an automated system. A private warning avoids public shaming, which can cause users to become defensive and escalate the conflict. A public warning or admonishment should be reserved for situations where a general reminder to the entire community is needed.

A good warning message is clear, concise, and non-confrontational. It should be a simple statement of fact, not an expression of personal disappointment. It must clearly state which piece of content was actioned, which specific rule was violated (ideally with a link to the guidelines), and what the consequence was. It should be written in a neutral, almost boilerplate tone. This depersonalizes the interaction, framing it as a standard procedural matter rather than a personal conflict between the user and the moderator.

If a user ignores warnings and continues their disruptive behavior, the next step on the ladder is a **Temporary Suspension**. Often called a "timeout" or a "mute," this action revokes the user's posting privileges for a set period. This serves two purposes. First, it immediately stops the user from causing further disruption. Second, it provides a mandatory cooling-off period, giving a heated user time to step away from their keyboard and reflect on their behavior. The length of a suspension can vary, typically starting with a short duration (e.g., 24 hours) for a first major offense and increasing for subsequent violations.

The final and most serious tool in the reactive moderation toolkit is the **Permanent Ban**. This action revokes a user's access to the community indefinitely. Banning is the digital equivalent of capital punishment and should be treated with appropriate gravity. For most violations, a ban should be the culmination of a clear escalation path: a user has been warned multiple times and perhaps temporarily suspended, yet continues to violate the rules. Their behavior demonstrates that they are either unable or unwilling to participate according to the community's standards.

However, some offenses are so severe that they warrant an immediate, non-negotiable permanent ban, bypassing all other steps. These "zero-tolerance" violations typically include posting illegal content (such as child exploitation material), making credible threats of violence, engaging in targeted hate speech, or deploying large-scale spam bots. In these cases, the immediate and permanent removal of the user is necessary to protect the safety and integrity of the community and the platform.

Once an action has been taken, whether it's a content removal or a ban, clear communication is essential. The user needs to know what happened and why. This reinforces the idea that moderation is not arbitrary. A boilerplate notification might read: "Your recent post, '[Quote from post],' was removed because it violated our community guideline against personal attacks. Please review our guidelines here before posting again. Continued violations may result in a temporary suspension of your account." This message is informative, direct, and avoids emotional language.

Thorough **Documentation** of all reactive moderation actions is non-negotiable. Most professional moderation software has built-in logging tools that automatically record what action was taken, which moderator took it, and at what time. Moderators should also add brief, objective notes to the log, explaining the reasoning behind their decision (e.g., "User was warned for same behavior on [Date]. Issuing 24-hour suspension."). This record-keeping is vital for several reasons. It ensures consistency among a team of moderators, provides a clear history if a user's behavior continues to escalate, and serves as the primary evidence when reviewing a user's appeal.

Moderators must also be prepared to handle abuse of the reporting system itself. Some users may engage in "weaponized reporting," where they mass-report a user they are arguing with, not for any legitimate rule violation, but simply as a form of harassment or to silence an opposing viewpoint. A skilled moderator learns to spot these patterns. When they see a dozen reports come in on a perfectly innocuous post, all at the same time, it's a red flag. Dealing with this requires investigating the reporters and potentially issuing warnings or sanctions against them for abusing the system.

Reactive moderation is often a thankless and emotionally taxing job. It involves constant exposure to the worst aspects of online behavior, from petty squabbles and spam to genuine hate and disturbing content. Moderators are the digital sanitation workers of the internet, cleaning up messes that others have made. This constant exposure to negativity can take a psychological toll, a topic that will be explored in greater depth later in this book. It requires a high degree of emotional resilience and the ability to remain objective and detached under pressure.

Ultimately, every reactive moderation action sends a message to the entire community. When members see that rules are enforced quickly and fairly, it reinforces their sense of safety and trust in the platform. They feel more confident that if they are targeted or if they encounter abusive content, the system will work to protect them. This confidence is the bedrock of a healthy community, and it is built one reactive moderation decision at a time. The work is often invisible when done well, but its impact is foundational.

CHAPTER SIX: Manual vs. Automated Moderation: Finding the Right Balance

In the early days of online communities, the very idea of automated moderation would have seemed like science fiction. Moderation was a purely artisanal craft, performed by a single forum owner or a small band of dedicated volunteers who read every post. As the internet grew from a small village into a sprawling megalopolis, this manual-only approach became untenable. The sheer volume of user-generated content created a mathematical problem: there are simply not enough human hours in the day to manually review the billions of comments, images, and videos uploaded daily. This challenge gave rise to the promise of automation—a way to manage the flood with the tireless efficiency of a machine.

This has created one of the central debates in community management: the perceived conflict between human moderators and automated systems. On one side, proponents of manual moderation champion the irreplaceable value of human nuance, empathy, and contextual understanding. On the other, advocates for automation point to the undeniable advantages of speed, scale, and consistency. The truth, however, is that framing this as a "versus" debate creates a false choice. The most effective, resilient, and scalable moderation strategies do not choose one over the other. Instead, they treat manual and automated moderation as two complementary tools in a single toolkit, forging a partnership that leverages the unique strengths of both.

Manual moderation is moderation with a human touch. It relies on the judgment, experience, and intuition of a person to interpret and enforce the community guidelines. The core strength of this approach lies in its sophisticated understanding of context, something that even the most advanced algorithms still struggle to replicate. A human moderator, particularly one who is an active member of the community, understands the group's history, its inside jokes, its recurring arguments, and the subtle relationships between its members.

This deep contextual knowledge allows a human to distinguish between a malicious personal attack and sarcastic banter between two old friends. They can recognize a new, coded slur that an automated filter, trained on last month's data, would miss entirely. Humans are adept at reading between the lines, discerning intent, and evaluating content not as a sterile collection of keywords but as a piece of communication within a dynamic social system. They can appreciate satire, understand irony, and know when a seemingly aggressive post is actually a quote from a popular movie the community loves.

Furthermore, manual moderation brings empathy to the enforcement process. When a user is confused about a rule or upset about a decision, a human moderator can engage with them, explain the reasoning with compassion, and de-escalate a potential conflict. This ability to communicate with nuance builds trust and reinforces the idea that moderation is being handled by reasonable people, not an unfeeling machine. It allows for flexibility and discretion. A human can choose to give a friendly, educational warning to a long-standing member who made a minor, out-of-character mistake, whereas a rigid automated system might issue a formal strike.

However, the weaknesses of a purely manual approach are significant and become more pronounced as a community grows. The most glaring limitation is its lack of scalability. A human moderator can only review a finite amount of content. As a platform scales to thousands or millions of users, it becomes physically and financially impossible to hire enough people to manually vet every single post. This means that response times for reported content can be slow, allowing harmful posts to remain visible for hours or even days, poisoning the environment before a moderator can get to them.

Inconsistency is another major challenge. Humans are not robots; their judgment can be influenced by fatigue, mood, or unconscious bias. Two different moderators, both acting in good faith, might look at the same borderline comment and come to two different conclusions. This can lead to the perception of unfair or biased enforcement, a sentiment that is highly corrosive to community trust. Finally, relying solely on manual moderation for all content, including the most toxic, exposes human moderators to a relentless stream of hate speech, graphic violence, and other disturbing material, creating a significant risk of psychological harm and burnout.

On the other side of the spectrum lies automated moderation, which uses software, algorithms, and artificial intelligence to screen content without direct human involvement. The primary advantage of this approach is its incredible speed and scale. An automated system can scan millions of pieces of content in the time it takes a human to read a single paragraph. It works 24 hours a day, 7 days a week, without needing breaks or sleep. This makes it an exceptionally powerful tool for dealing with high-volume, low-complexity violations.

The most basic form of automation involves simple keyword and phrase filters. These systems can be configured to automatically block or flag posts containing known slurs, profane language, or links to spam websites. More sophisticated systems use hashing technology, creating a unique digital fingerprint for an image or video. This is highly effective for automatically detecting and removing known illegal content, such as Child Sexual Abuse Material (CSAM), or copyrighted media, by comparing the hash of a new upload against a database of known prohibited content.

Modern automated systems are increasingly powered by machine learning and AI. These tools can go beyond simple keyword matching to analyze patterns and perform tasks like sentiment analysis to gauge the emotional tone of a comment. They can identify and block spam bots by detecting non-human behavior, such as posting at an impossible speed or using repetitive language. For a large platform, this kind of automation isn't just helpful; it's an absolute necessity. It serves as a crucial first line of defense, catching a huge percentage of obvious violations before they ever reach the community or a human moderator's queue.

Despite its power, automation is a blunt instrument when used in isolation. Its greatest weakness is its profound lack of contextual understanding. An algorithm trained to flag the word "kill" cannot distinguish between a credible death threat, friends arranging a game of "kill the carrier," or someone enthusiastically exclaiming, "That comedian absolutely killed it on stage!" This leads to the frustrating problem of false positives, where perfectly legitimate content is mistakenly flagged or removed, angering users and stifling conversation. The infamous "Scunthorpe problem," where the English town's name was historically blocked by filters because it contains an embedded profane substring, is a classic example of this contextual blindness.

Automated systems also struggle to keep up with the creativity of malicious actors. When a new slur or a hateful meme emerges, bad actors can spread it widely before developers have a chance to update their filters or retrain their AI models. Users intent on causing harm will constantly innovate, using coded language, symbols, and alternate spellings to evade detection. Furthermore, AI models are only as good as the data they are trained on. If that data contains inherent biases, the AI will learn and even amplify those biases, potentially leading to the disproportionate flagging of content from certain dialects or demographic groups.

Given the clear strengths and weaknesses of each approach, it becomes obvious that the optimal solution is not to choose one, but to blend them. The most effective moderation framework is a hybrid model where humans and machines work in partnership, each covering for the other's weaknesses. This strategy is often referred to as the "Centaur" model, named after the mythological creature that combined the intelligence of a human with the power of a horse. In this model, the machine provides the speed and scale, while the human provides the judgment and nuance.

In a typical Centaur workflow, automation acts as a wide-net filter and a triage nurse. The automated systems scan all incoming content in real-time. A large portion of content will be obviously acceptable and will be allowed through without any intervention. Another portion will contain clear, high-confidence violations— such as a known spam link or a racial slur—and the system can automatically take an action, such as removing the content and issuing a warning or suspension. This instantly handles the most obvious and voluminous rule-breaking, freeing up human attention for more complex issues.

The true power of the hybrid model lies in how it handles the content in the middle: the gray-area cases where the algorithm is uncertain. Instead of making a definitive call and risking a false positive, the automated system flags the content and routes it to a human moderation queue for review. This allows the human moderators to focus their finite time and cognitive energy on the posts that actually require human intelligence. They are no longer searching for needles in a haystack; the machine has brought them a neat pile of potential needles to examine.

This creates a powerful feedback loop. When a human moderator reviews a piece of content flagged by the AI and makes a decision—either confirming the violation or overriding the flag— that decision can be fed back into the system. This is a form of active learning. By providing the AI with a steady stream of corrected examples, its model becomes smarter and more accurate over time. A moderator teaching the machine that a certain phrase, in a certain context, is not a violation helps the system make a better prediction the next time it encounters a similar situation.

The specific balance between manual and automated moderation is not a universal constant. It must be tailored to the specific needs, resources, and risk profile of each community. For a very small, niche hobby forum run by a single volunteer, a purely manual approach might be perfectly sufficient. The volume of content is low, and the community's culture is well understood by the moderator. There is little need for a complex and expensive automated system.

Conversely, a massive social media platform or a popular online game with millions of daily users simply cannot function without heavy reliance on automation. For these platforms, the question is not *if* they should automate, but *how* they should automate. They will typically employ a multi-layered system, with automation handling the first pass on all content, routing different types of potential violations to specialized teams of human moderators who are trained to handle specific issues like hate speech, disinformation, or child safety.

The type of content being shared is another critical factor. A text-only forum has different needs than a live-streaming video platform. Moderating a live video stream is one of the most intense challenges in the field, as harm can occur in real-time. Here, automated tools that can detect nudity, violence, or other violations in the video feed itself are essential for providing moderators with alerts that allow them to intervene instantly.

Ultimately, the goal is to design a system that is both effective and efficient. Automation should be used to handle the predictable and the voluminous. Manual moderation should be reserved for the ambiguous, the sensitive, and the novel. By finding the right balance, a community can create a moderation system that is fast, consistent, and scalable, without sacrificing the crucial human elements of empathy, context, and sound judgment. The machine becomes the tireless sentinel, and the human becomes the thoughtful judge.

CHAPTER SEVEN: Leveraging AI-Powered Moderation Tools

The hybrid model of moderation, where human intelligence is augmented by the raw power of computation, hinges on the quality of its automated half. While the previous chapter established the conceptual balance between manual and automated approaches, this chapter delves into the engine that powers modern, large-scale automation: Artificial Intelligence. The simple keyword filters of the past have given way to sophisticated AI-powered systems capable of understanding, seeing, and detecting patterns in ways that were once the exclusive domain of the human brain. Leveraging these tools effectively is no longer a luxury for the largest platforms; it is an increasingly essential component of responsible community management at any significant scale.

At its heart, AI-powered moderation is the application of machine learning (ML) and its sub-disciplines to the task of content analysis. Unlike a simple filter that is explicitly programmed to block a static list of words, a machine learning model is "trained" on vast datasets of content. It learns to recognize complex patterns associated with different types of content, much like a human learns from experience. This allows it to make predictions about new, unseen content. The primary branches of AI used in this field are Natural Language Processing (NLP) for text, Computer Vision for images and video, and behavioral analysis for user activity patterns. These technologies form the core of the modern moderation toolkit.

For text-based communities, Natural Language Processing is the foundational technology. NLP gives a machine the ability to read and, to a certain extent, comprehend human language. This goes far beyond just spotting forbidden words. One of the most common applications of NLP is **Sentiment Analysis**, where the AI is trained to gauge the emotional tone of a piece of text. It can classify a comment as positive, negative, or neutral. This can be a powerful, if coarse, first-pass filter. A sudden spike in highly negative comments in a particular thread can act as an early warning system for moderators, alerting them to a potential "flame war" or a contentious issue that requires their attention before it escalates.

Building upon this is **Toxicity and Profanity Detection**. Advanced models in this area are not just looking for a list of swear words. They are trained on millions of examples of online comments that have been labeled by humans as toxic, abusive, or profane. This allows them to understand the contextual difference between a user saying "this is a piece of junk" in a product review and "you are a piece of junk" as a personal attack. These systems can assign a toxicity score to a comment, allowing for more granular rules, such as automatically flagging anything above a 75% toxicity score for human review while allowing less severe comments through.

AI also excels at **Topic and Intent Classification**. A model can be trained to recognize the purpose of a post. For example, it can learn to distinguish between a user asking a question, a user providing product feedback, a user posting spam, and a user harassing someone else. This is invaluable for workflow automation. An AI can automatically route all posts classified as "support questions" to a customer service queue, send all "feedback" posts to a product team's channel, and send all posts flagged as "harassment" directly to a high-priority human moderation queue. This sorting process saves countless hours of manual triage.

The fight against hate speech is one of the most complex areas where NLP is applied. Malicious actors constantly invent new slurs and "dog whistles"—coded language that seems innocuous to an outsider but carries a hateful message for a specific in-group. While AI can be trained to detect known slurs, it struggles with these novel and evolving terms. However, it can identify patterns of association. If a new, seemingly innocent phrase consistently appears alongside known hateful symbols or in discussions that get flagged for hate speech, the AI can learn to associate that new phrase with a high probability of being a violation, flagging it for human experts to investigate.

The visual world of images and videos presents a different set of challenges, addressed by the field of **Computer Vision**. AI models can be trained to "see" and interpret the content of an image or a video frame. The most fundamental application of this is **NSFW (Not Safe For Work) Detection**. Models are trained on enormous datasets of images labeled as pornographic, graphically violent, or otherwise adult in nature. When a user uploads a new image, the system can analyze it and assign a probability score for it being NSFW, allowing it to be blocked or blurred automatically pending human review.

Computer Vision also powers **Object and Scene Recognition**. This allows an AI to identify specific objects within an image, such as weapons, drug paraphernalia, or hateful symbols like swastikas. This is a crucial tool for enforcing policies against the promotion of illegal activities or hate speech, which are often communicated visually rather than through text. A user might post a picture of a weapon with a threatening caption; even if the text itself evades filters, the image analysis can flag the post for review.

A particularly insidious challenge in content moderation is text hidden within images, a common tactic used to circumvent text-based filters. A user might post a hateful message as a screenshot of text or an internet meme. This is where **Optical Character Recognition (OCR)** becomes vital. OCR is a technology that allows the AI to read the text embedded in an image file. By integrating OCR into the moderation workflow, an image can be scanned not only for its visual content but also for any text it contains, which can then be fed into the same NLP models used to analyze regular comments.

Moderating video, especially live-streaming video, is an even greater challenge due to the sheer volume of data. AI can analyze a video stream frame by frame to detect visual policy violations. More efficiently, it can analyze the audio track, transcribing the spoken words into text that can be processed by NLP models in near real-time. This allows for the automatic flagging of moments in a live stream where a user says something that violates hate speech or harassment policies, creating a timestamped event that a human moderator can immediately jump to and review.

Beyond analyzing the content of a single post, AI can also perform **Behavioral Analysis**, looking at the patterns of a user's activity over time. This is one of the most effective methods for detecting spam and inauthentic behavior. A human user, for example, cannot post 200 identical comments across a platform in the span of 30 seconds. An AI can immediately recognize this non-human pattern of behavior and flag or ban the account as a potential bot without ever needing to analyze the content of the comments themselves.

This extends to detecting **Coordinated Inauthentic Behavior**, a more sophisticated form of platform manipulation. This occurs when a network of seemingly independent accounts works in concert to spread disinformation or harass a target. An AI can analyze the relationships between accounts, identifying groups that were all created around the same time, post on the same niche topics with similar language, and consistently amplify each other's content. While one of these accounts might look normal in isolation, the AI can see the suspicious network-level pattern and flag the entire cluster for investigation by a human analyst.

Behavioral analysis can also be used to generate a **User Reputation Score**. An AI can build a profile of a user based on their history. Factors might include the age of the account, the number of times their content has been positively engaged with (liked, upvoted), and, most importantly, the number of times their content has been flagged and confirmed as a violation. A new account with a history of having its posts deleted for spam could be assigned a low reputation score. This score can then be used to inform moderation policy. For instance, posts from users with very low reputation scores could be automatically held in a queue for human approval before they become public.

The practical implementation of these tools usually revolves around a confidence-based triage system. When an AI model analyzes a piece of content, it doesn't return a simple "yes" or "no" verdict. Instead, it produces a **Confidence Score**, a statistical probability that the content violates a specific policy. For example, it might determine there is a 98% probability that an image contains graphic violence, a 70% probability that a comment is toxic, and a 20% probability that a post is spam.

This scoring system allows for the creation of a sophisticated, multi-tiered workflow. Content where the AI has extremely high confidence in its assessment (e.g., >95% probability of being a known CSAM image) can be handled with full automation—the content is removed, and the user is banned without human intervention. This is reserved for the most clear-cut, zero-tolerance violations.

Content that falls into a middle range of confidence (e.g., a 60% to 95% probability) is where the human-machine partnership truly shines. The AI is not sure enough to act on its own, so it routes the content to a queue for a human moderator to make the final judgment. This ensures that the limited and valuable time of human moderators is spent on the ambiguous, context-dependent cases where their intelligence is most needed. They are not bogged down by the obvious spam or the clearly acceptable content.

Content with a low confidence score (e.g., <60%) is typically allowed to pass through without interruption. This system of thresholds is the key to balancing the speed of automation with the accuracy of human judgment. The specific percentages can be tuned and adjusted over time based on the platform's tolerance for risk and the observed accuracy of the AI models.

Crucially, this workflow creates a continuous **Feedback Loop**. When a human moderator reviews a piece of content that the AI flagged and either confirms or overturns the AI's prediction, that decision is valuable data. This data is fed back into the system to retrain the machine learning model. If moderators consistently tell the AI that it is incorrectly flagging a certain term as toxic, the model will eventually learn to lower the toxicity score it assigns to that term. This process, often called "human-in-the-loop" machine learning, allows the AI to become progressively smarter and more attuned to the specific nuances of a particular community over time.

Despite their power, it is imperative to understand the inherent limitations and risks associated with AI moderation tools. The most significant is the **Nuance Gap**. AI struggles profoundly with the subtleties of human communication. It is notoriously bad at detecting sarcasm, irony, satire, and parody. It can be easily confused by evolving slang, regional dialects, and complex cultural references. An AI trained primarily on American English might incorrectly flag common phrases from other English-speaking cultures as profane or abusive. This lack of true understanding means it will always be a step behind human creativity.

This leads directly to the **Bias Problem**. Machine learning models are a reflection of the data they are trained on. If the initial dataset used to train a toxicity model contains historical biases—for example, if content from certain minority groups was disproportionately labeled as toxic by human reviewers in the past—the AI will learn and codify those biases. This can lead to the creation of a system that unfairly and systematically penalizes certain demographics, all while appearing to be objective. Mitigating this algorithmic bias requires a conscious and ongoing effort in curating diverse and representative training data and constantly auditing the model's performance across different user groups.

Furthermore, moderators are in a constant battle against **Adversarial Actors** who are actively trying to deceive the AI. Users will replace letters with similar-looking numbers or symbols (e.g., "h4te"), add extraneous punctuation to words, or embed hateful text in a visually "noisy" meme to confuse OCR systems. This creates a perpetual arms race, where developers must constantly update their models to counter the latest evasion techniques, and the AI must be retrained to recognize these new patterns.

Finally, when deciding how to integrate these tools, organizations face the classic **Build vs. Buy** dilemma. Building a proprietary, in-house AI moderation system offers maximum customization but requires an enormous investment in specialized talent and resources. For most companies, the more practical option is to "buy" a solution by partnering with a third-party moderation AI vendor. When evaluating these vendors, it is crucial to ask about language support, the types of content they can analyze, the ease of API integration, and, most importantly, how they allow you to customize the models and rules to fit the unique culture and guidelines of your community. A one-size-fits-all AI is rarely a perfect fit for anyone.

CHAPTER EIGHT: Building and Training Your Moderation Team

An online community, in its infancy, can often be managed by a single passionate individual. This founder, creator, or community manager acts as the sole architect, host, and security guard. They write the rules, greet the newcomers, and handle any troublemakers. But as a community grows, this solo act becomes unsustainable. The sheer volume of content, the need for round-the-clock coverage across different time zones, and the ever-present risk of burnout create a clear and urgent need for reinforcements. The moment one person can no longer reasonably read every post or respond to every report in a timely manner is the moment to start building a team. A moderation team is the community's immune system, and scaling it effectively is critical for long-term health.

The first fundamental decision is whether to build a team of volunteers, paid professionals, or a hybrid of the two. There is no single right answer, as the best choice depends entirely on the community's nature and resources. Volunteer moderators are the backbone of a vast portion of the internet, from Reddit subreddits to hobbyist forums and fan-run Discord servers. They are typically drawn from the ranks of the community's most passionate and dedicated members. Their primary motivation is not financial but intrinsic: a genuine desire to protect a space they care about. This passion is their greatest strength, providing a level of dedication and intrinsic community knowledge that is difficult to buy.

The downside of a volunteer model is that, by its nature, you cannot place the same demands on volunteers as you can on employees. Their availability may be inconsistent, life events can pull them away without notice, and there is a limit to the amount of tedious or emotionally taxing work you can reasonably ask them to do for free. Managing a volunteer team requires a leadership style built on inspiration, appreciation, and shared purpose rather than top-down authority.

Paid moderation, on the other hand, is the standard for businesses, brands, and large-scale platforms. Professional moderators are accountable, can be required to work specific shifts to ensure 24/7 coverage, and can be held to stringent performance metrics. This model offers reliability and control. The trade-off is the significant financial cost and the fact that a paid moderator, especially one from a third-party service, may not have the same deep-seated cultural understanding of the community they are protecting. They moderate according to a rulebook, but they may miss the unwritten social norms that a long-standing member innately understands. For many, a hybrid model offers the best of both worlds, with a core team of paid community managers leading and supporting a larger group of dedicated volunteers.

Once the model is chosen, the recruitment process begins. The single best place to find potential moderators is almost always within the community itself. Your future leaders are likely already there, acting as unofficial moderators in their daily interactions. These are the "super users" or "helpers"—the members who consistently welcome newcomers, patiently answer questions, constructively correct misinformation, and gently guide conversations back on track when they start to stray. They model the desired behavior not because they have to, but because it is their nature.

Identifying these individuals requires careful observation. Look for members who demonstrate patience in the face of frustration and who can disagree with others respectfully. Pay attention to who the community naturally turns to for help or information. These individuals have already earned a degree of trust and social capital, which will be invaluable when they step into a formal moderation role. Actively seeking out these members and inviting them to apply is often more effective than simply putting out a public "help wanted" post, which can attract individuals motivated by a desire for power rather than a desire to serve.

The next step is to formalize the application and vetting process. Even for volunteers, having a structured process is crucial for setting expectations and ensuring fairness. A simple application form can ask for basic information, such as their timezone and general availability, but should focus on situational questions. Avoid generic queries like "Why do you want to be a moderator?". Instead, ask for specific examples: "Describe a time you saw a conflict in the community. How would you have handled it?" or "Link to a post or comment you've made that you feel is a good example of a helpful contribution."

The review of a candidate's post history is the single most important part of the vetting process. It is their resume, reference check, and interview all rolled into one. Does the candidate have a clean record of following the community guidelines themselves? You cannot have an enforcer who is also a frequent rule-breaker. How do they communicate when they disagree with someone? Do they resort to sarcasm or personal attacks, or do they engage with arguments calmly and rationally? A history of respectful disagreement is a powerful positive indicator. Look for a pattern of helpfulness, maturity, and a temperament that remains steady under pressure.

Following this review, a more direct conversation—an informal interview, even via text—is essential. This is the time to present hypothetical scenarios that test their judgment in the gray areas. "A popular, long-time member makes a joke that is borderline offensive. A new user reports it. What are your next steps?" There is no single correct answer to a question like this, but their thought process is revealing. A good candidate will talk about gathering context, considering the intent versus the impact, and weighing the member's history against the need to make the newcomer feel safe. A poor candidate will jump to an extreme, absolutist decision without asking for more information. This conversation is also your chance to screen for red flags, such as an "us versus them" attitude toward the user base or an eagerness to wield the banhammer.

As the team begins to form, a clear structure becomes necessary to prevent confusion and ensure efficiency. A flat hierarchy where every moderator has the same permissions and authority can work for very small teams, but as the group grows, defining roles and responsibilities is key. A tiered system can be highly effective. For instance, you might have Junior Moderators whose primary role is to review the reporting queue, remove obvious spam, and flag more complex cases for senior team members. Senior Moderators could have the additional ability to issue warnings and temporary suspensions. Finally, Administrators or the Community Manager would handle the most serious issues, such as permanent bans, policy decisions, and user appeals. This structure provides a clear path for escalation and allows you to grant new moderators limited permissions while they are still learning the ropes.

The single most critical piece of infrastructure for a moderation team is a private communication channel. This is the team's digital headquarters, a secure back-end space—be it a private Slack, a locked forum, or a dedicated Discord server—where they can work together. This is where moderators can ask for a second opinion on a difficult case, discuss emerging patterns of disruptive behavior, and coordinate their response to a large-scale incident. It is the forum for debate that ensures consistent policy application. Without this hub, moderators are left to operate in isolated silos, which inevitably leads to inconsistent enforcement and a fragmented team culture. This space is also vital for building team camaraderie and providing mutual support, which is essential for mitigating the stress of the role.

With a team selected and a structure in place, the next stage is comprehensive training and onboarding. Simply handing a new moderator a set of keys and a copy of the public guidelines is setting them up for failure. Effective training goes much deeper, equipping them not just with the rules, but with the processes, tools, and philosophy of moderation specific to your community. This begins with the creation of an internal "Moderator Handbook." This confidential document is the team's operational manual. It should contain the public guidelines, but also expand on them with internal-only clarifications, examples of common edge cases, and the specific rationale behind each rule.

The handbook should also detail the team's standard operating procedures. This includes a step-by-step guide to the moderation workflow: how to claim a ticket from the queue, the investigative steps to take, the precise wording of warning templates, how and when to use the suspension and ban tools, and, crucially, how to document every action taken. Providing standardized templates for warnings and other communications is vital. It ensures that all users receive the same clear, neutral, and professional messaging, regardless of which moderator is handling their case. This reduces the chance of a user feeling singled out and personalizing the conflict.

Training must include a hands-on walkthrough of the moderation tools. A new recruit needs to be completely comfortable with the platform's backend interface before they are expected to use it under pressure. They should know how to view a user's moderation history, how to properly log an action, and how to use any integrated AI or automation tools the team relies upon. A mistake made due to unfamiliarity with the software can have significant consequences for a user, so this technical proficiency is non-negotiable.

Perhaps the most valuable part of the onboarding process is a mentorship or shadowing period. Pair a new moderator with a seasoned veteran for their first couple of weeks. During this time, the trainee can "shadow" the active moderation queue. Their task is not to take action, but to observe reported content and state what action they *would* take and why. The senior moderator can then review their reasoning, either affirming their decision or gently correcting their course. This provides a safe, supervised environment for the new moderator to apply their training to real-world scenarios and calibrate their judgment against that of an experienced team member.

Once a moderator is fully onboarded, the process of building the team is not over; it has merely transitioned into a process of ongoing management and development. Regular team meetings, whether via text or voice, are essential for keeping everyone aligned. These meetings are a chance to discuss recent challenging cases, calibrate on gray-area interpretations of the guidelines, and share information about new trends in the community or new tactics being used by malicious actors. This is also the time to discuss potential changes to the guidelines, ensuring that the rules evolve with the community they are meant to serve.

To maintain fairness and high standards, some form of quality review is necessary. This doesn't need to be an intimidating performance review, but rather a collaborative process. A team lead or a peer can periodically review a sampling of a moderator's recent actions from the logs. The goal is to ensure consistency and identify any areas where a moderator might need additional coaching or where a policy itself may be unclear. The discovery that three different moderators handled three identical situations in three different ways is not a sign of individual failure; it is a sign of a policy that needs to be clarified for everyone.

Finally, leading a moderation team means trusting and empowering them. Once they are trained and have proven their judgment, it is vital to avoid micromanagement. Give them the autonomy to make decisions within the established framework. A moderator who feels their every action is being second-guessed will quickly become hesitant and demoralized. Create a culture of support where it is safe to ask questions and even to admit to making a mistake. A well-built, well-trained, and well-supported moderation team is more than a group of rule enforcers; it is a cohesive unit that acts as the collective guardian of the community's culture and its future.

CHAPTER NINE: Handling Trolls, Spam, and Malicious Behavior

Up to this point, our focus has largely been on managing the behavior of well-intentioned community members who may occasionally, and often accidentally, stray from the guidelines. We have discussed how to handle disagreements, off-topic posts, and minor infractions with an educational and corrective approach. Now, we must turn our attention to a different class of user entirely: the malicious actor. These are the individuals and groups who do not come to participate in good faith. Their goal is not to contribute, but to disrupt, exploit, or harm the community and its members. Handling these actors requires a shift in mindset from that of a community gardener to that of a security professional. The objective is no longer to nurture, but to identify, contain, and remove threats as swiftly and efficiently as possible.

This category of behavior encompasses a range of activities, but three of the most common and disruptive are trolling, spamming, and other explicitly malicious acts like harassment and doxxing. While their methods may differ, their defining characteristic is intent. The user who misunderstands a rule is a teachable moment; the user who intentionally breaks a rule to provoke a reaction is a security threat. Recognizing the difference is a crucial skill for any moderator, as applying a gentle, corrective approach to a determinedly malicious actor is not only ineffective but can often make the situation worse.

The term "troll" is one of the most overused and misunderstood in the online lexicon. It is often misapplied to anyone who voices a dissenting or unpopular opinion. This is a critical distinction to make: someone who disagrees with the community consensus is not a troll; someone who posts in bad faith to deliberately derail conversation is. A troll's primary currency is attention, and their goal is to elicit an emotional response. They feed on the anger, frustration, and confusion of others. They are the arsonists of the conversational world, seeking to set fires and watch the chaos unfold from a safe distance.

The motivations behind trolling are varied and complex, a subject we will touch upon again in the chapter on psychology. For some, it is a cure for boredom. For others, it is a way to feel a sense of power or control in an otherwise powerless-feeling life. Some trolls derive sadistic pleasure from upsetting others, while others may be ideologically motivated, seeking to silence or disrupt communities they oppose. Regardless of the reason, the moderator's response should be guided by a single, unyielding principle: the troll's motivation is irrelevant. Spending time trying to understand or reason with a troll is a waste of resources and plays directly into their hands.

The first step in dealing with a troll is to accurately identify their behavior. Trolls are often skilled at operating in the gray areas of community guidelines, crafting posts that are inflammatory and disruptive without technically violating a specific, explicit rule. This requires moderators to look for patterns of behavior, not just individual posts. One common tactic is "sea-lioning," a form of bad-faith questioning where the troll feigns ignorance and relentlessly demands evidence for even the most basic claims, not to learn, but to exhaust the patience of other participants.

Another tell-tale sign is "goalpost shifting." In a debate, a troll will ignore any evidence presented to them and simply change the criteria for what they will accept as proof. No amount of data or reasoned argument will ever satisfy them because their goal is not to be convinced, but to keep the argument going. Similarly, some engage in the "Gish Gallop," a technique where they overwhelm an opponent with a sheer number of individually weak or irrelevant arguments, making it impossible to respond to everything and thus creating the illusion of having "won" the debate.

Perhaps the most insidious form of trolling is "concern trolling." Here, the troll will pretend to be a supporter of the community or an idea, but will voice "concerns" that are actually designed to sow doubt and discord. For example, in a support group for a social cause, a concern troll might say, "I completely support our mission, but I'm worried that our recent protests are making us look too aggressive and are alienating potential allies." The statement is framed as helpful advice, but its underlying purpose is to demoralize the group and undermine its strategy.

Once a pattern of trolling is identified, the response must be swift, decisive, and devoid of emotion. The cardinal rule, known across the internet for decades, is simple: "Do not feed the trolls." Engaging a troll in an argument is giving them exactly what they crave. It validates their tactics, gives them a platform, and draws more attention to their disruptive behavior. A public argument between a moderator and a troll is a victory for the troll, every single time, as it derails the community and makes the moderation team appear flustered.

The correct approach is a quiet, surgical removal of the problem. This typically follows a simple, low-drama process. The first step is to remove the trolling content. The posts should be deleted without any public comment or explanation in the thread itself. The goal is to erase the disruption as if it never happened, allowing the normal conversation to resume as quickly as possible. This is not about censorship; it is about sanitation.

Simultaneously, the moderator should engage their standard escalation ladder, but often on an accelerated timeline. While a normal user might get a gentle reminder and then a warning, a user clearly identified as a troll may receive a single, firm warning or proceed directly to a temporary suspension. Any communication with the troll regarding this action must be done privately, through direct message or email. This communication should be brief, boring, and procedural. It should quote the broken rule, state the action taken, and provide a link to the guidelines. There should be no emotion, no argument, and no debate. A simple "Your posts were removed for violating our policy against trolling. Continuing this behavior will result in a ban," is sufficient.

In many cases, the troll will respond to this private message, attempting to draw the moderator into the argument they were denied in public. They will claim they were misunderstood, that the moderation is unfair, or that their freedom of speech is being oppressed. It is absolutely critical to resist the urge to engage in this debate. The decision has been made. The moderator can either ignore the reply entirely or respond with a single, final message, such as, "The decision is not open for debate. Any further violations will result in a permanent ban."

For persistent trolls, a permanent ban is the final solution. In some cases, moderators may employ a more advanced technique known as a "shadowban" or "hellban." In this scenario, the banned user is not notified of the ban. They can still log in, write posts, and submit comments, but this content is invisible to everyone else on the platform except for themselves and the moderators. From the troll's perspective, everything seems normal; they are simply being ignored. This can be a highly effective tactic, as the troll may continue to post into the void for days or weeks without realizing they have been neutralized, preventing them from immediately creating a new account to continue their disruption. However, this method can be technically complex to implement and raises ethical questions about transparency.

Where trolls attack the social fabric of a community, spammers attack its infrastructure. Spam is the digital equivalent of junk mail: unsolicited, irrelevant, and often deceptive content posted in bulk. While some spam is relatively harmless advertising, much of it is far more sinister, involving phishing scams designed to steal user credentials, or links to websites that install malware on a visitor's computer. A community that is overrun with spam quickly becomes unusable and appears neglected, driving away legitimate users.

Fighting spam is a fundamentally different challenge than handling trolls. A troll requires psychological insight; spam requires technical defenses. This is one area where automated moderation tools are not just helpful, they are indispensable. The sheer volume of spam, much of it generated by automated bots, makes manual removal an impossible task. The most effective anti-spam strategy is a layered defense that begins before the spammer can even create an account.

The first layer of defense is at the registration gate. Requiring new users to complete a CAPTCHA ("Completely Automated Public Turing test to tell Computers and Humans Apart") is a standard and effective way to block simple bots from signing up. Requiring email verification, where a user must click a link sent to their email address to activate their account, adds another barrier that thwarts many automated scripts.

A highly effective proactive technique is to implement a probationary period for new accounts. For example, a new user's first one to three posts might be held in an approval queue, requiring a moderator to manually approve them before they go public. Spammers want immediate results, and this delay is often enough of a deterrent to make them move on to an easier target. Similarly, you can place limitations on new accounts, such as disallowing them from posting links or images until they have made a certain number of approved text-only posts. This prevents the common hit-and-run spammer who registers an account only to post a single malicious link.

Even with these defenses, some spam will get through. Identifying it is usually straightforward. The content is often completely unrelated to the community's topic. It may contain tell-tale phrases like "make money fast" or "100% free download." The grammar is often poor, and the message will almost always feature a link, sometimes hidden with a URL shortener to disguise its true destination. A single user posting the same or similar messages across multiple threads is another red flag.

The response to spam should be immediate and absolute. There are no warnings and no second chances. The moment a spam account is identified, the moderator should use a tool that allows them to permanently ban the user account and simultaneously delete all content that account has ever posted in a single action. This is a purely janitorial task; there is no need for communication with the banned account.

Beyond individual trolls and spammers, moderators must also be prepared to handle other, more targeted forms of malicious behavior. One of the most serious is "doxxing," the act of researching and broadcasting a user's private, personally identifiable information (PII) without their consent. This can include their real name, home address, phone number, place of employment, or private photos. Doxxing is a severe violation of privacy that can lead to real-world harassment, job loss, and even physical danger for the victim. Every community must have a zero-tolerance policy for this behavior. Any content containing doxxed information must be removed immediately, and the user who posted it must be permanently banned without discussion.

Harassment and stalking represent a more sustained form of malicious conduct. While a personal attack may be a one-off insult in a heated argument, harassment is a persistent and targeted campaign of abuse against a specific individual. This can involve a user repeatedly sending abusive private messages, following a victim from thread to thread to insult their posts, or creating multiple accounts to continue the abuse after being blocked. This is another area where documentation is key. Moderators must take reports of harassment seriously, review the post history of the accused user to identify the pattern of behavior, and take decisive action to protect the target. This often means banning the harasser and providing the victim with information on how to use platform tools to block any future accounts the user might create.

Finally, communities can be targeted by "brigading" or "coordinated raids." This is when a group of users, often organized in an outside community (like a different subreddit or a private chat group), descends on a particular thread or community en masse. Their goal is to disrupt conversations, downvote all content from community members, upvote their own content to dominate the space, and harass the community's members. This can feel like a sudden invasion. Identifying a brigade involves spotting a sudden, unnatural influx of new or inactive accounts all appearing in the same thread and pushing the same viewpoint. The response requires a coordinated effort from the moderation team. It often involves locking the targeted threads, setting the community to a temporary "restricted" mode where only established members can post, and performing a mass ban of the accounts identified as part of the raid.

Dealing with the full spectrum of malicious behavior is one of the most stressful and demanding aspects of moderation. It requires vigilance, a thick skin, and the ability to act decisively and dispassionately. It is also where a well-trained team, backed by robust tools and clear policies, proves its worth. Every piece of spam removed, every troll banned, and every victim of harassment protected is a direct contribution to the safety and long-term health of the community. It is the difficult but essential work that makes positive engagement possible.

CHAPTER TEN: Conflict Resolution and De-escalation Techniques

Not all fires are set by arsonists. While the previous chapter focused on dealing with malicious actors who intentionally seek to harm the community, a far more common and delicate challenge for any moderator is the conflict that erupts between well-intentioned members. These are not trolls or spammers; they are passionate participants who, through a combination of strongly held beliefs and the inherent limitations of text-based communication, find themselves locked in a cycle of escalating hostility. Healthy debate is the lifeblood of many communities, but when it devolves into personal attacks and flame wars, it can poison the well for everyone. The moderator's role in these situations is not that of a security guard ejecting an intruder, but that of a skilled diplomat and mediator, tasked with the subtle art of de-escalation.

Understanding the anatomy of these conflicts is the first step toward resolving them. Unlike a troll's manufactured outrage, conflict between genuine members typically stems from a real disagreement. The subject matter could be anything: a debate over the best way to tune an engine, a fierce disagreement about the strategic choices in a video game, or a clash of interpretations over a film's ending. The passion that makes these individuals valuable community members is the same energy that can fuel the fire of conflict. The problem is rarely the disagreement itself, but the way in which it is expressed.

The digital environment is a natural incubator for misunderstanding. When you strip away body language, tone of voice, and facial expressions, all that remains are the words on the screen. A sarcastic comment intended as a lighthearted jab can easily be read as a vicious insult. A terse, quickly typed reply can be interpreted as dismissive and arrogant. This ambiguity, known as context collapse, means that participants often project the worst possible intent onto the words of others, creating a feedback loop where each reply becomes more defensive and more aggressive than the last. The argument shifts from being about the topic to being about the perceived disrespect between the participants.

The moderator's primary objective in these situations is not to declare a winner in the underlying debate. It is a fatal error for a moderator to take sides on the substance of the argument, even if they have a strong personal opinion. Doing so instantly destroys their credibility as a neutral arbiter and transforms them from a referee into just another player on the field. The goal is singular: to lower the emotional temperature of the conversation and guide it back to a constructive, or at least civil, state. The health of the community takes precedence over the specific outcome of any single debate.

Knowing when to intervene is an art form honed by experience. Stepping in too early can stifle a vigorous and productive debate, making members feel like they are being coddled or that dissenting opinions are unwelcome. This can create a chilling effect where people become afraid to express strong views. Intervening too late, however, allows the conflict to fester and grow, driving away bystanders and creating lasting factions and resentments within the community. The key is to learn to recognize the tipping point—the moment a discussion transitions from a passionate debate about ideas into a toxic series of attacks against people.

There are several key indicators that signal the need for moderator intervention. The most obvious is the appearance of explicit rule violations, such as clear name-calling, insults, or ad hominem attacks. Another red flag is a shift to absolutist language and a refusal to acknowledge any part of the other person's argument. The conversation ceases to be an exchange of ideas and becomes a series of repetitive, entrenched monologues. You may also notice other, uninvolved members starting to comment on the tone of the discussion ("Can we all just calm down?") or leaving the thread entirely. This is a sign that the conflict is no longer contained and is beginning to damage the experience for the wider community.

Once the decision to intervene has been made, the moderator must approach the situation with a carefully chosen set of tools designed to de-escalate, not inflame. The first and most important tool is the moderator's own tone. A calm, professional, and impartial demeanor is critical. If a moderator enters a heated thread with an aggressive or condescending attitude, it will only pour gasoline on the fire. Your public-facing actions should model the behavior you wish to see from the community members.

A gentle, low-impact first step is often to post a **Neutral Reminder** in the thread. This is a public comment that does not single out any specific user but reminds everyone of the relevant community guidelines. It can be as simple as, "As a friendly reminder to everyone participating in this discussion, please remember to keep the conversation civil and focus on debating the topic, not each other. You can review our guideline on respectful conduct here." This serves as a gentle course correction that gives the participants a chance to self-regulate without feeling publicly admonished.

If the conflict is more advanced, a more direct approach may be needed. This involves **Acknowledging and Validating** the passion of the participants while simultaneously reframing the conversation. A moderator might post something like, "I can see that this is a topic that many of you feel very strongly about, and we appreciate the passionate discussion. However, the tone has become more personal than we'd like. Let's try to step back from the heated language and refocus on the core issues." This type of message validates the members' emotional investment, which can make them more receptive to the request to change their behavior. It shows you are listening, not just policing.

Sometimes, the best tactic is to actively try to **Find Common Ground**. After reading the thread, a moderator can step in and highlight areas of agreement that may have been lost in the heat of the moment. "This has been a very intense debate, but it seems like both @UserA and @UserB agree that the initial problem is X, even if you disagree on the best solution. Could we explore that shared understanding a bit more?" This technique can short-circuit the adversarial dynamic by reminding the participants that they are members of the same community with shared interests, not mortal enemies.

When a thread has become hopelessly derailed and toxic, one of the most effective tools is to enforce a **Cooling-Off Period**. This involves a moderator making a public post and then locking the thread from further replies. The post should be clear and transparent: "This discussion is no longer productive and has devolved into personal attacks. We are locking this thread for 24 hours to give everyone a chance to cool off. Please use this time to step away from the keyboard. We will re-evaluate reopening the thread tomorrow." This action immediately stops the conflict and provides a much-needed circuit breaker for the participants' anger.

While public interventions are powerful, some situations are best handled privately. If one or two specific individuals are consistently responsible for escalating the conflict, contacting them via private message or direct message (DM) is often the most effective approach. This avoids the public shaming that can make a user defensive and double down on their behavior. A private message allows for a more direct and frank conversation about their conduct.

The key to a successful private message is to focus on specific behaviors, not on the user's personality or intent. Instead of saying, "You are being aggressive and rude," which is an attack on their character, say, "Your last three comments in that thread included personal insults, which is a violation of our community guidelines." Quote their own words back to them if necessary. This frames the issue as a matter of concrete, observable actions that have consequences, rather than a subjective judgment of their character. End the message by clearly stating the required change in behavior and the potential consequences if it continues (e.g., a temporary suspension).

In cases where a thread contains a mix of substantive debate and a few deeply problematic, rule-breaking comments, **Surgical Content Removal** is a valuable technique. Instead of deleting the entire thread, a moderator can carefully remove only the specific comments that contain personal attacks or other violations. When doing so, it is crucial to leave a public moderation note in place of the removed comment (e.g., "[Comment removed by moderator for a personal attack]"). This maintains the flow of the conversation for other readers while making it clear that an enforcement action was taken. It is a precise intervention that cleans up the mess without destroying the entire structure.

Sometimes, despite a moderator's best efforts at de-escalation, the participants are unable or unwilling to stop. In these cases, the moderator must escalate their own actions. The first step is often **Locking the Thread** permanently, with a final post explaining that since the participants could not adhere to the community guidelines, the discussion is now closed. If the behavior continues in other threads, the moderator must then transition from conflict resolution to rule enforcement, issuing formal warnings and, if necessary, temporary suspensions to the individuals who are perpetuating the toxic behavior. This should always be a last resort, but it is a necessary one to protect the health of the overall community.

The work does not end once the immediate conflict has been quenched. The aftermath requires careful management. It can be helpful to **Follow Up** privately with the main participants a day or two later, especially if they are long-standing members in good standing. A simple, "Hey, just wanted to check in and make sure things are okay. I know that discussion got heated, but I hope we can move forward," can go a long way toward repairing hurt feelings and reassuring the member that they are still valued.

The moderation team should also conduct a post-mortem on any major conflict. Was there something about the topic that was uniquely divisive? Is there a feature of the platform that encourages this kind of conflict? Most importantly, is there a community guideline that is unclear or is consistently being "sea-lioned" in bad-faith arguments? A recurring conflict around a specific topic might indicate the need for a pinned FAQ post to address common misunderstandings, or even a new, more specific rule. Each conflict, while painful in the moment, is a learning opportunity that can be used to make the community more resilient in the future.

Resolving disputes between community members is one of the most challenging aspects of moderation because it requires a delicate balance of authority, empathy, and strategic communication. It is a deeply human problem that cannot be solved by algorithms alone. By acting as calm, neutral mediators, moderators can transform a potentially destructive confrontation into a resolved disagreement, reinforcing the community's standards and demonstrating that it is possible to disagree passionately without being disagreeable.

CHAPTER ELEVEN: The Legal Landscape of Content Moderation

For a long time, the internet was romanticized as a new frontier, a digital Wild West beyond the reach of dusty old laws made for the physical world. This was, and remains, a dangerous misconception. The internet is not a separate reality; it is an extension of our own, and the same legal principles that govern society apply to the content posted, shared, and debated within online communities. For a moderator, understanding the broad strokes of this legal landscape is not about becoming a lawyer. It is about recognizing the difference between a simple rule violation and a potential legal firestorm. It is about knowing when a situation has moved beyond the scope of community management and into the realm of legal compliance, where a wrong step can have serious consequences for the platform, its users, and even the moderator themselves.

Navigating this terrain is complicated by the fact that the law is often several steps behind technology. Courts and legislatures are constantly playing catch-up, trying to apply centuries-old concepts like defamation and copyright to a world of memes, live streams, and global, instantaneous communication. The result is a patchwork of laws that vary dramatically from one country to the next. What is considered protected free speech in one jurisdiction might be a criminal offense in another. This global complexity means that platforms, and by extension their moderation teams, must act as the frontline interpreters and enforcers of a complex and ever-shifting legal reality.

Perhaps one of the most common legal issues that moderators will encounter is **Copyright Infringement**. In simple terms, copyright is a legal right that grants the creator of an original work—be it a photo, a song, an article, or a piece of software—exclusive control over how that work is used and distributed. When a user uploads a full-length movie, a watermarked stock photograph, or a licensed piece of music without permission, they are likely infringing on the creator's copyright. A community that becomes a haven for this kind of activity, known as piracy, can face significant legal and financial penalties.

In the United States, the governing legislation for this issue is the Digital Millennium Copyright Act (DMCA), passed in 1998. The DMCA includes a critical provision known as a "safe harbor." This provision essentially states that an online service provider (like a community platform) is not liable for the copyright-infringing actions of its users, provided it meets certain conditions. The most important of these conditions is that the platform must establish a clear "notice-and-takedown" system. This means they must provide a way for copyright holders to formally report infringing content and must act expeditiously to remove that content once a valid notice is received.

The moderator's role in this process is procedural, not judicial. When a DMCA takedown notice arrives, the moderator's job is not to determine whether copyright was actually infringed. That is a legal question for a court to decide. Their job is simply to verify that the takedown notice is properly formatted and contains all the required information, and then to remove the specified content. The user who posted the content is then typically notified and given the opportunity to file a "counter-notice" if they believe their use of the material was legitimate (for instance, under "fair use" provisions). The platform is the intermediary, following a legally prescribed script to maintain its safe harbor protection.

Another minefield is **Defamation**. Defamation is the act of communicating a false statement about someone that harms their reputation. When it is in written form, as it almost always is online, it is called libel. A user who posts, "My former boss John Smith is an embezzler," when in fact John Smith is not, could be sued for libel. The critical question for the platform is whether it can be held responsible for publishing that user's defamatory statement. This is a point of major divergence in international law and will be a central theme of the next chapter on Section 230.

In the United States, platforms are granted broad immunity from liability for most user-generated content, including defamatory statements. In many other parts of the world, however, the legal protections for intermediaries are far weaker. In the United Kingdom and many other countries, a platform can be considered a "publisher" and can be held liable for libelous comments made by its users if it is notified of the comment and fails to remove it in a timely manner. This has led to a phenomenon known as "libel tourism," where individuals may choose to sue in a country with more plaintiff-friendly defamation laws, regardless of where the platform or the user is based. For global communities, this means that a cautious approach to reports of defamation is often the wisest course.

The area where law, culture, and platform policy collide most intensely is around **Hate Speech and Harassment**. From a legal perspective, the definition of hate speech varies enormously across the globe. The United States, with its First Amendment, provides very broad protections for speech, and the legal bar for what constitutes illegal hate speech is extremely high. Generally, for speech to be illegal, it must cross the line into direct incitement to imminent violence or constitute a "true threat." A post that is merely offensive, racist, or bigoted, while reprehensible, is often legally protected speech in the US.

Contrast this with the legal situation in many European countries. Germany's Network Enforcement Act (Netzwerkdurchsetzungsgesetz, or NetzDG) requires large social media platforms to remove "manifestly illegal" content, including hate speech, within 24 hours of receiving a report, or face massive fines. The German criminal code has a much broader definition of illegal hate speech, including "incitement to hatred" against population groups. This means a post that is legally permissible in the United States could be a criminal offense if viewed by a user in Germany.

Because of this legal fragmentation, most major platforms have created community guidelines on hate speech that are far more restrictive than what is legally required in their home country.

They do this for two reasons: first, to create a single, globally enforceable policy that helps them comply with the laws of multiple countries simultaneously; and second, to foster a welcoming environment that is not actively hostile to a majority of their user base. This is a critical concept for moderators to grasp: the vast majority of content removed for "hate speech" is removed for violating platform policy, not for breaking a specific law.

While the definition of hate speech is variable, the law is much more consistent when it comes to **True Threats and Incitement to Violence**. A "true threat" is a statement that a reasonable person would interpret as a serious expression of intent to commit an act of unlawful violence against a particular individual or group. A post saying, "I am going to bring a weapon to City Hall tomorrow," is not a debate about policy; it is a potential threat that falls outside of any free speech protection. Similarly, content that directly incites or encourages others to commit imminent acts of violence is illegal in almost every jurisdiction. Such content must be removed immediately, and in cases where the threat is specific and credible, platforms often have a legal and ethical duty to report the information to law enforcement.

Beyond speech, moderators must be vigilant for content that is, in itself, illegal to possess or distribute. The most serious and non-negotiable category of this is **Child Sexual Abuse Material (CSAM)**. There is no gray area here. The possession and distribution of CSAM is a serious felony in virtually every country on earth. Platforms have an absolute legal and moral obligation to remove this content immediately upon discovery and report it to the relevant authorities. In the United States, this means reporting it to the National Center for Missing & Exploited Children (NCMEC). Many platforms use automated hashing technology, like PhotoDNA, which can detect known CSAM images and videos at the moment of upload, preventing them from ever reaching the community and automatically triggering the reporting process. A moderator who encounters potential CSAM should never attempt to investigate on their own; their sole responsibility is to follow the platform's strict protocol for immediate internal escalation and reporting.

Similarly, content that promotes or facilitates **Terrorism** is also subject to strict legal controls. Regulations in the European Union, for example, can require platforms to remove terrorist content within one hour of being notified by authorities. This includes material produced by designated terrorist organizations, as well as content that provides instruction on making explosives or carrying out attacks. Like CSAM, this content is subject to a zero-tolerance policy.

Finally, communities must have policies in place to prohibit the use of the platform for **Illegal Commerce**. This means forbidding users from posting content that facilitates the sale of illegal drugs, firearms (in violation of local laws), counterfeit goods, or other regulated products. While a single post might not seem like a major issue, a community that gains a reputation as an unregulated marketplace for illegal goods will inevitably attract the attention of law enforcement agencies.

This global patchwork of laws creates an immense **Jurisdictional Challenge**. A community may be hosted on servers in Ireland, owned by a company in California, moderated by a volunteer in India, and be populated by users from Brazil and Germany. Whose laws apply? The answer is often "all of the above." Courts have increasingly taken the view that a platform is subject to the laws of the country where its content is accessible. This means a post that is legal in its country of origin can still be subject to a court order for removal in a country where it is deemed illegal.

Rather than trying to apply hundreds of different legal standards to different users, most global platforms create a single, universal Terms of Service and set of Community Guidelines that all users must agree to. This is the platform's own private law. The Terms of Service (ToS) is a legally binding contract between the user and the platform. By signing up, the user agrees to abide by the platform's rules. This contract gives the platform the legal right to remove content or ban a user for any reason that violates the ToS, even if the content itself is perfectly legal. A user may have a legal right to say something under the First Amendment, but they do not have a right to say it on a privately owned platform if it violates the rules they agreed to. This is the legal foundation for all moderation actions.

A final, and understandable, concern is the question of a moderator's own **Personal Liability**. Can a volunteer moderator be sued for removing a post or banning a user? In general, the risk is extremely low. When moderators are acting as agents of the platform and are enforcing established policies in good faith, they are typically shielded by the same legal protections that cover the platform itself. The lawsuit would be directed at the company, not the individual moderator. However, this protection relies on the moderator acting within the scope of their training and the platform's policies. A "rogue" moderator who goes far outside the guidelines to harass a user or delete content for purely personal reasons could, in a rare and extreme case, expose themselves to some level of risk.

The legal landscape of content moderation is a dense and often intimidating subject. However, by understanding the fundamental categories of risk—copyright, defamation, hate speech, illegal content—and the critical role of the Terms of Service as the ultimate source of authority, moderators can learn to identify potential legal issues effectively. Their role is not to be a judge or jury, but to be a vigilant and informed first responder, protecting the community and the platform by consistently enforcing the rules they are entrusted to uphold.

CHAPTER TWELVE: Understanding Section 230 and Intermediary Liability

In the entire legal code of the United States, there are few provisions that have had a more profound and controversial impact on the shape of the modern internet than a small piece of legislation known officially as Section 230 of the Communications Decency Act of 1996. Often referred to simply as "the twenty-six words that created the internet," this law is the fundamental legal pillar upon which the practice of online community moderation in the U.S. is built. To understand why you can remove a user's post for violating your community guidelines without your company being sued for everything else that user has ever said, you must first understand the concept of intermediary liability and the legal paradox that Section 230 was created to solve.

At its core, the question of intermediary liability is simple: when a person uses a service to harm someone else, who is responsible? If someone uses the postal service to mail a threatening letter, we do not hold the post office legally liable. If someone uses a telephone to commit fraud, the phone company is not sued. In these cases, the services are seen as neutral conduits, or "common carriers," with no control over how they are used. But what about a service that hosts and displays content for millions to see? Is it a neutral conduit like the phone company, or is it more like a newspaper, which is legally responsible for every word it prints, from the front-page headline to the smallest classified ad? This was the central question facing the burgeoning online world of the early 1990s.

Before Section 230, the courts tried to answer this question by applying old media laws to the new digital landscape, and the results created a crippling dilemma for anyone trying to run an online community. The first landmark case was *Cubby, Inc. v. CompuServe Inc.* in 1991. CompuServe hosted a number of online forums, one of which contained defamatory statements about a company called Cubby. Cubby sued CompuServe, arguing that

CompuServe was the publisher of the defamatory content. The court disagreed, ruling that CompuServe was merely a distributor, not a publisher. Because CompuServe exercised no editorial control over the content in the forum, the court found it was analogous to a bookstore, which could not be expected to have read every book on its shelves and therefore could not be held liable for their contents. This ruling set a clear precedent: do not moderate content, and you will be protected from liability.

This precedent was turned on its head four years later in the 1995 case of *Stratton Oakmont, Inc. v. Prodigy Services Co.* The brokerage firm Stratton Oakmont (the same firm depicted in the film *The Wolf of Wall Street*) sued the online service Prodigy over defamatory comments made by a user on one of its message boards. Unlike CompuServe, Prodigy had marketed itself as a family-friendly service and actively moderated its forums to enforce content guidelines. The court seized on this fact. It ruled that because Prodigy did engage in moderation, it was exercising editorial control. Therefore, it was acting as a publisher, not a mere distributor, and could be held liable for the defamatory content it failed to remove.

Together, these two cases created an impossible situation for online platforms, a catch-22 that became known as the "moderator's dilemma." The law effectively told platforms: "If you touch nothing, you are safe. But if you try to clean up your service even a little bit, you become legally responsible for every single thing your users post." This created a perverse incentive to do nothing—to allow forums to fill up with spam, hate, and libel rather than risk the catastrophic liability that came with trying to be a responsible platform owner. It was a legal framework that actively punished good-faith moderation.

It was in this climate that Congress passed the Communications Decency Act in 1996. While the act was primarily an attempt to regulate indecency online (a goal that was later found unconstitutional by the Supreme Court), it contained a small but revolutionary provision drafted by Representatives Chris Cox and Ron Wyden. This provision, Section 230, was designed specifically to solve the moderator's dilemma. It did so with two key clauses.

The first and most famous clause is Section 230(c)(1), which contains the celebrated "twenty-six words": "`No provider or user of an interactive computer service shall be treated as the publisher or speaker of any information provided by another information content provider.`" To understand this, we need to break it down. An "interactive computer service" is a broad term that covers everything from a massive social media network to a small community forum or even the comments section on a blog. An "information content provider" is the person who actually creates the content—the user who writes the comment or uploads the video.

The crucial phrase is "shall not be treated as the publisher or speaker." This language directly overturns the legal reasoning used in the *Prodigy* case. It establishes that, for the purposes of liability, a platform hosting third-party content is not the publisher of that content. It is a legal shield that separates the platform from the actions of its users. If a user posts something defamatory, illegal, or otherwise harmful, the legal responsibility lies with the user— the information content provider—not with the interactive computer service that hosted it. This is the core of the liability shield.

However, if the law had stopped there, it would only have reinforced the *CompuServe* precedent, encouraging platforms to take a hands-off approach. This is where the second key clause, Section 230(c)(2), comes into play. Often called the "Good Samaritan" provision, it states that a platform cannot be held liable for any action "voluntarily taken in good faith to restrict access to or availability of material that the provider or user considers to be obscene, lewd, lascivious, filthy, excessively violent, harassing, or otherwise objectionable, whether or not such material is constitutionally protected."

This second clause is the part of the law that explicitly empowers and protects the act of moderation. It directly addresses the moderator's dilemma by saying, in essence, "Not only are you not liable for your users' content, but you are also not liable for the decisions you make to remove that content." It gives platforms a legal right to moderate as they see fit, according to their own standards of what is "otherwise objectionable," without the fear that this act of moderation will transform them into a publisher with all the attendant liabilities. It broke the paradox and created a legal framework where platforms were free to moderate as much or as little as they wanted without fear of litigation.

It is equally important to understand what Section 230 does not do. The shield is broad, but it is not absolute. The law contains several key exceptions. Most notably, it offers no protection against federal criminal liability. If a platform is itself being used to commit federal crimes, and the platform owners are complicit, Section 230 does not apply.

Furthermore, the law explicitly exempts intellectual property law. This is why copyright infringement is handled under the separate legal framework of the DMCA, as discussed in the previous chapter. A platform cannot use Section 230 to ignore valid DMCA takedown notices for pirated content.

Over the years, the law has been amended. The most significant change came in 2018 with the passage of the Fight Online Sex Trafficking Act (FOSTA) and the Stop Enabling Sex Traffickers Act (SESTA). This legislation carved out a new exception to Section 230, stating that the liability shield does not apply to civil claims or state criminal charges related to the online promotion or facilitation of sex trafficking. This change made platforms potentially liable for user-generated content that falls into this specific category, representing a major shift in the law's scope.

For the day-to-day work of a community moderator, Section 230 is the silent, often invisible, legal architecture that makes their job possible. It is the reason why platforms can create and enforce a Terms of Service that goes far beyond the baseline of the law. A user's post might be legally protected speech under the First Amendment, but if it violates the community's rule against personal attacks, Section 230 protects the platform's right to remove it. It affirms that the First Amendment prevents the government from censoring speech, but it does not compel a private company to host speech that it finds objectionable on its own platform.

Without Section 230, the internet as we know it—a vibrant, chaotic, and endlessly creative space dominated by user-generated content—would likely not exist. The legal risk would be too great. Platforms would be forced into one of two extremes: either a sanitized, heavily-policed environment where all content is pre-screened by lawyers, killing real-time conversation; or a completely unmoderated free-for-all, abandoned to the worst impulses of its users. The law created the middle ground where moderated communities can flourish.

In recent years, this foundational law has become the subject of intense political debate from all sides of the spectrum. Critics, often from the political right, argue that large technology companies have used the protection of Section 230 to engage in politically biased censorship. Their argument is that by making editorial decisions about what content to promote, demote, or remove, these platforms are in fact acting as publishers and should not be entitled to the law's protections. They contend that the liability shield is being used to silence certain viewpoints with impunity.

From the political left, a different set of criticisms has emerged. These critics argue that Section 230 provides a "get out of jail free" card that allows platforms to profit from harmful content— such as hate speech, harassment, and dangerous disinformation— without facing any liability for the real-world damage that content causes. They argue that the broad immunity removes the financial incentive for companies to invest adequately in safety and moderation, and that reforming the law would force platforms to be more responsible stewards of their digital spaces.

Meanwhile, defenders of the law, a diverse coalition of technology companies, digital rights organizations, and free speech advocates, argue that Section 230 remains as essential today as it was in 1996. They contend that repealing or significantly weakening the law would have devastating consequences. The threat of constant litigation, they argue, would force platforms to become hyper-cautious, leading them to aggressively remove any remotely controversial content. This would not only stifle speech but would also disproportionately harm smaller startups and online communities that lack the financial resources and legal teams to fight endless court battles, thus further entrenching the dominance of the largest players.

It is also crucial to remember that Section 230 is a uniquely American law. The rest of the world has taken very different approaches to intermediary liability. The European Union, for instance, has moved toward a model of co-regulation with its Digital Services Act (DSA). The DSA does not offer a blanket liability shield in the same way as Section 230. Instead, it imposes a detailed set of obligations on platforms, requiring them to have transparent and robust processes for content moderation, risk assessment, and user appeals. This global divergence in legal philosophy presents a significant challenge for communities that operate across international borders, a topic we will explore in a later chapter.

For the moderator on the front lines, the swirling political debates about the future of Section 230 can feel distant and abstract. But the principles it established are woven into the fabric of every moderation decision. The law is what grants a private community the authority to be its own governor, to set its own standards, and to enforce them without having to answer for the infinite variety of content its users might create. It is the legal engine that powers the very concept of a curated online community.

CHAPTER THIRTEEN: Navigating Privacy Concerns and Data Protection (GDPR)

In the course of their duties, a moderator is granted access to a privileged view of the community. They see behind the curtain, accessing a range of user data that is invisible to the average member. This access is not a perk of the job; it is an essential part of the toolkit required to keep the community safe and functional. However, this necessity creates a fundamental tension with one of the most significant and rapidly evolving principles of the digital age: the user's right to privacy. The act of moderation requires the processing of user data, while a growing body of law strictly governs how that data can be collected, used, and stored. For the modern moderator, being an effective guardian of the community now also means being a responsible steward of its data.

The data a moderator interacts with goes far beyond the public-facing content of posts and comments. To effectively investigate a report or identify a pattern of abuse, a moderator may need access to a user's IP address to check for ban evasion through multiple accounts. They might need to see the email address associated with an account to cross-reference it with known spammers. They will certainly need to view a user's entire posting history, including any previously deleted content or warnings, to make an informed decision about an escalation. In some cases, depending on the platform's policies and the severity of the issue, they may even need to review content from private messages that has been reported by a recipient. Each piece of this data is a tool, but it is also a piece of someone's personal information, entrusted to the platform.

For decades, the handling of this data was largely at the discretion of the platform owner, governed by little more than a loosely written privacy policy. That era has decisively ended. The global legal landscape has shifted dramatically toward recognizing data privacy as a fundamental human right. This shift was crystallized by the implementation of the European Union's General Data Protection Regulation (GDPR) in May 2018. The GDPR is not just another piece of obscure European bureaucracy; it is a landmark piece of legislation whose impact is felt by any online community with a global audience. Its principles have become the gold standard for privacy law, inspiring similar legislation around the world.

The reach of the GDPR is its most critical feature to understand. It is not limited to companies based in the EU. The law's "territorial scope" is expansive, applying to any organization, anywhere in the world, that processes the personal data of individuals who are located in the European Union. If your community for classic car enthusiasts is based in Chicago but has even a single member from Germany, you are subject to the GDPR with respect to that member's data. For virtually any community of scale, this means that complying with GDPR is not optional; it is a baseline requirement for operating on the global internet.

To navigate this landscape, moderators do not need to become lawyers, but they do need to understand the core concepts that underpin the law. The first is the definition of "Personal Data." The GDPR defines this very broadly as any information relating to an identified or identifiable natural person. This is far more than just a name and address. It includes online identifiers like a username, an email address, a user ID number, and an IP address. It can even include the content a person writes if it reveals information about them. For moderation purposes, it is safest to assume that almost all of the user-specific information you handle qualifies as personal data.

Under the law, the organization that runs the community (the company, the non-profit) is considered the "Data Controller." The controller is the entity that determines the purposes and means of processing personal data. The individual moderators, whether paid staff or volunteers, are acting as agents of the controller. They are the hands that carry out the work, but the ultimate responsibility for compliance rests with the organization. This is why it is so critical for the organization to provide its moderators with clear policies and training on how to handle data correctly.

The GDPR requires that all processing of personal data be justified by a "lawful basis." You cannot simply collect and use data for any reason you see fit. While "consent" is the most well-known lawful basis, for the purposes of moderation, the most relevant basis is often "legitimate interests." This means the processing is necessary for the legitimate interests pursued by the data controller, provided those interests are not overridden by the rights and freedoms of the individual. In this context, a platform has a clear legitimate interest in keeping its community safe from spam, harassment, and illegal content. The processing of user data to enforce community guidelines and the Terms of Service is a necessary part of pursuing that interest.

This legal framework gives rise to a set of powerful rights that the GDPR grants to all users. A moderator needs to be aware of these rights, not because they will be the one to fulfill them, but because they are often the first point of contact for a user trying to exercise them. The moderator's role is to recognize the request and escalate it according to the platform's established procedure.

The first is the **Right of Access**. A user can submit a formal request to the platform asking for a copy of all the personal data that is held about them. This is often called a Data Subject Access Request (DSAR). The response to a DSAR can include everything from their account details and IP logs to the internal notes a moderator has made about their past conduct.

Next is the **Right to Rectification**. If a user believes the platform holds inaccurate personal data about them, they have the right to have it corrected. This is typically less relevant for moderation data, which is usually a record of behavior, but it is a core right nonetheless.

The most famous and often most challenging right is the **Right of Erasure**, more popularly known as the "Right to be Forgotten." This allows a user, under certain circumstances, to request the deletion of their personal data. This right is not absolute and is where the needs of the community can clash directly with the rights of the individual. A user might demand that not only their account be deleted, but that every post they have ever made be scrubbed from the community's history. They might also demand that any record of their past warnings or bans be erased.

Fulfilling such a request completely can have unintended consequences. Deleting all of a user's posts could render years of valuable community discussions incoherent, leaving gaping holes in conversations that other users contributed to. Deleting a ban record could allow a malicious actor to simply sign up for a new account and continue their disruptive behavior, as the moderation team would have no memory of their past offenses. Because of this, platforms often argue that they have a legitimate interest in retaining certain data, even after a user has left. They might fulfill an erasure request by anonymizing the user's public posts—replacing their username with a generic tag like "[Deleted User]"—while retaining the moderator-facing records for a limited and clearly defined period for security purposes. The exact policy for handling these requests must be carefully defined by the platform's legal and privacy teams.

These legal principles have direct, practical implications for the day-to-day work of a moderator. The first and most important is the duty of **Confidentiality**. The moderator's access to user data is a sacred trust. Any personal information a moderator sees—an email address, an IP address, the content of a reported private message—is strictly confidential. It must never be shared publicly or discussed outside of the secure, private channels designated for the moderation team. Sharing a user's private information as a way to "win" an argument or to shame a troublemaker is not just a policy violation; it is a serious data breach that could have legal consequences for the platform and the moderator.

This is why the secure, internal communication channel discussed in a previous chapter is so critical. It is the only appropriate place to discuss a specific user's case and share the data necessary to make a decision. A conversation that happens in an unsecured, public-facing space, even one that seems private, poses an unacceptable risk.

Moderators must also be trained on the platform's specific **Data Handling Procedures**. When a user sends a message saying, "I want to exercise my right to be forgotten under GDPR," the moderator's job is not to debate the merits of the request. Their job is to know the exact, step-by-step process for escalating that request to the designated Data Protection Officer (DPO) or the privacy team responsible for handling it. Having a clear, well-documented internal process is the key to ensuring these legally significant requests are handled correctly and in a timely manner.

The principle of **Data Minimization**—collecting and retaining only the data that is absolutely necessary for a specific purpose—also has an impact on moderation. This gives rise to the need for a **Data Retention Policy**. How long should a moderator's notes on a user be kept? How long should a record of a temporary suspension be stored? There is no single answer, but the platform must define a policy. Retaining these records indefinitely could be seen as a violation of data minimization. A common approach is to set a rolling time frame, for example, stating that moderation records will be deleted two years after an account becomes inactive. This allows the team to identify long-term patterns of abuse while ensuring that data is not kept forever.

While the GDPR is the most comprehensive, it is by no means the only privacy law a community might face. The global trend is toward more data protection, not less. In the United States, the California Consumer Privacy Act (CCPA) and its successor, the California Privacy Rights Act (CPRA), grant California residents a similar set of rights to access and delete their data. Other countries, from Brazil (LGPD) to Canada (PIPEDA), have their own comprehensive privacy laws. The moderator does not need to know the details of every single law. They simply need to understand the underlying principles of data protection and recognize that users around the world are being empowered with new rights over their information.

Ultimately, navigating the world of data privacy requires a shift in perspective. A moderator is more than just an enforcer of social norms; they are a frontline data steward. They are entrusted with sensitive information, and their handling of that information is a direct reflection of the platform's respect for its users. A breach of privacy, whether through carelessness or malice, can destroy a community's trust far more quickly and permanently than any troll or flame war. Respecting user privacy is not a bureaucratic hurdle to be overcome; it is a core component of building a safe and trustworthy community.

CHAPTER FOURTEEN: The Psychology of Online Behavior

To effectively manage a community, one must understand not only the rules of the platform but also the strange and often counterintuitive rules of the human mind as it operates in a digital space. The internet is not a neutral conduit for communication; it is a psychological environment with its own unique properties, an environment that can subtly and profoundly alter how we perceive ourselves and interact with others. People who are perfectly reasonable and empathetic in face-to-face interactions can transform into aggressive, intolerant combatants when placed behind a keyboard. This is not because the internet magically creates bad people, but because it systematically removes many of the social and psychological guardrails that govern our behavior in the physical world. For a moderator, understanding these underlying psychological mechanics is like a meteorologist understanding atmospheric pressure; it allows you to see the invisible forces that shape the weather of your community.

The central concept for understanding this transformation is the **Online Disinhibition Effect**, a term coined by the psychologist John Suler. It describes the well-documented phenomenon where people feel freer to say and do things online that they would not ordinarily say or do in a real-world, face-to-face setting. This is the root cause of both the best and worst of online behavior. This disinhibition is not inherently negative. Suler identified two distinct types. **Benign Disinhibition** is when this newfound freedom leads to positive outcomes. People may feel more comfortable sharing deeply personal feelings, revealing hidden vulnerabilities, or expressing unusual kindness and generosity to strangers, secure in the anonymity of the digital space. This is the force that allows online support groups to flourish, where individuals can discuss sensitive topics with a candor they might never achieve with their own family.

The other side of the coin, and the one that occupies a great deal of a moderator's time, is **Toxic Disinhibition**. This is when the same lack of restraint leads to antisocial behavior: rude language, harsh criticism, anger, hatred, and threats. It is the engine that powers flame wars, harassment campaigns, and trolling. Understanding that these two seemingly opposite behaviors stem from the same psychological root is crucial. The same environment that can foster incredible support can, if left unmanaged, just as easily foster incredible toxicity. Suler identified six main factors that work in concert to create this effect. For a moderator, these six factors are the psychological ingredients of almost every conflict they will have to manage.

The first and most powerful of these factors is **Dissociative Anonymity**. On many platforms, a user is known only by a pseudonym or a username. This creates a psychological separation, a dissociation between their online persona and their real-world identity. The actions of "DragonSlayer42" can feel psychologically distinct from the actions of John Smith, the accountant and father of two. This disconnect from one's real name and reputation can significantly lower the perceived consequences of one's actions. If no one knows who you are, you are less likely to be held accountable by your employer, your family, or your community for what you say. This is not just about avoiding punishment; it's about the freedom that comes from acting as a different, untethered version of oneself.

Closely related is **Invisibility**. In most online interactions, you cannot see the person you are communicating with. You cannot see their facial expression, their body language, or the look of hurt in their eyes when you post an insulting comment. This physical invisibility removes a massive channel of non-verbal feedback that we rely on in real-world conversations to modulate our own behavior. Without these cues, it is much easier to dehumanize the person on the other side of the screen. They cease to be a flesh-and-blood person with feelings and become just a block of text, an avatar, an abstract opponent. This lack of visual presence makes it far easier to be aggressive, as you are not confronted with the immediate, visible impact of your words.

The third factor is **Asynchronicity**. Many online communications, particularly on forums and social media, do not happen in real-time. A user can post a comment—perhaps a particularly nasty one—and then simply walk away from their computer. They do not have to deal with the immediate, in-the-moment reaction of the other person. This is the digital equivalent of a "hit-and-run." The time lag between messages allows a person to fire off an emotional salvo without having to endure the immediate conversational consequences. This lack of real-time feedback loop can encourage more impulsive and less considered communication, as the sender does not have to engage in the difficult work of navigating an immediate emotional response.

Perhaps the most subtle and psychologically complex factor is **Solipsistic Introjection**. This is a fancy term for a very common experience. When you read another person's text, you are not hearing their voice; you are hearing the words in your own voice, inside your own head. In the absence of real-world cues about what the other person is actually like—their tone, their demeanor—we unconsciously cast them as a character in our own internal drama. We project our own hopes, fears, and unresolved issues onto the blank canvas of their text. This can lead to profound misunderstandings. A person might read a simple, direct question in an angry and accusatory tone because they themselves are feeling defensive, transforming a neutral interaction into a hostile one before the other person has even had a chance to clarify.

Fifth is **Dissociative Imagination**. The combination of anonymity and the text-based nature of the internet can make online spaces feel less like a part of real life and more like a game or an alternate reality. This can create a sense that the rules of normal social interaction don't apply, and that the actions taken within this "game" do not have real-world weight. People might engage in extreme behavior, from elaborate scams to vicious character assassinations, with a sense of detachment, as if they are simply playing a role. The community becomes a fantasy space where they can act out impulses that are normally suppressed, all under the subconscious belief that "this isn't real life."

The final factor is the **Minimization of Authority**. In the physical world, authority is often communicated through visual and environmental cues: a police officer's uniform, a judge's robes, the impressive architecture of a government building. Online, these cues are absent. A moderator's username might be a different color, and they may have a title under their name, but in the flattened, text-based hierarchy of the internet, they are still just another person behind a screen. This can lead users to perceive authority figures as less legitimate or powerful than they would in real life. They may feel more emboldened to challenge, insult, or ignore a moderator's instructions because the psychological weight of their authority is greatly diminished.

Beyond the disinhibition effect, several common cognitive biases are amplified in online environments and act as constant sources of friction. One of the most pervasive is the **Fundamental Attribution Error**. This is the tendency to attribute other people's negative actions to their character or personality, while attributing our own negative actions to external, situational factors. For example, if another user makes a typo, we might think, "This person is uneducated or careless." If we make a typo, we think, "I was typing too quickly on my phone." In an online debate, this means we are predisposed to believe that the person who disagrees with us is not just wrong, but is a bad, stupid, or malicious person. This bias is a primary driver of the ad hominem attacks that moderators must constantly clean up.

This is often compounded by **Confirmation Bias**, the natural human tendency to seek out, interpret, and favor information that confirms our pre-existing beliefs. Online communities, especially those centered on a specific interest or ideology, can easily become "echo chambers" or "filter bubbles" where dissenting opinions are rare and the group's shared beliefs are constantly reinforced. When someone from outside this bubble enters the conversation with a contrary viewpoint, the community members are not only predisposed to disagree, but their confirmation bias can make the opposing view feel like a personal attack on their identity and their group, leading to an immediate and hostile reaction.

The online world is also a perfect petri dish for the **Dunning-Kruger Effect**, a cognitive bias wherein people with low ability in a particular domain tend to overestimate their competence. The internet provides a platform for anyone to present themselves as an expert on any given topic. In a specialized community, this can lead to situations where a novice confidently gives incorrect and sometimes dangerous advice, and then reacts with extreme hostility when corrected by genuine experts. Their lack of knowledge makes them unable to recognize their own incompetence, and they interpret the correction not as helpful guidance but as an unwarranted personal attack.

These individual psychological tendencies are further amplified by the dynamics of the group itself. Social Identity Theory helps explain how this works. It posits that a person's sense of self is partly derived from their membership in social groups. When an individual identifies strongly with an online community—be it a group for fans of a particular TV show, supporters of a political cause, or players of a video game—they begin to see that group as an "in-group." The success and status of the in-group become tied to their own self-esteem.

The natural consequence of forming a strong in-group is the creation of "out-groups." These are the other communities, the rival fandoms, the opposing political factions, or simply the rest of the uninitiated internet. The stronger the identification with the in-group, the greater the potential for prejudice and hostility toward the out-group. This can manifest as anything from playful rivalry to outright brigading and harassment. Moderators of highly cohesive communities must be constantly aware of this dynamic, as the same group loyalty that makes the community strong can also be the source of its most toxic external behavior.

This can lead to a powerful and dangerous phenomenon known as **Deindividuation**. This is a psychological state where an individual's sense of personal identity and responsibility is diffused by their immersion in a group. When they are part of a large, anonymous online mob, they can feel a diminished sense of accountability for their actions. The group's identity temporarily replaces their own. This is the psychological mechanism behind online pile-ons and witch hunts, where hundreds or thousands of people, most of whom would never engage in such behavior individually, feel empowered to join in a collective campaign of harassment. They are no longer a person; they are simply a part of the angry mob.

For a moderator, these psychological principles are not just abstract theories; they are diagnostic tools. Understanding them provides a framework for interpreting the seemingly irrational behavior they encounter daily. When a user lashes out with a surprisingly aggressive comment, a moderator who understands solipsistic introjection might consider that the user may have misinterpreted the tone of a previous post, rather than simply concluding that the user is a jerk. When a flame war erupts, a moderator who understands the fundamental attribution error can see it not just as two people fighting, but as a predictable clash of cognitive biases.

This understanding does not excuse bad behavior, but it does inform the response. It encourages a moderation style that is less about punishment and more about skillful intervention. It can guide a moderator to choose a de-escalation technique that addresses the underlying psychological driver of the conflict. It allows them to anticipate problems, to recognize the early warning signs of an echo chamber solidifying, or to spot the patterns of a user who is beginning to treat the community like a video game. Ultimately, moderating an online community is a form of applied psychology. The code and the guidelines provide the structure, but a deep understanding of human nature is what allows a moderator to transform a simple collection of users into a genuine community.

CHAPTER FIFTEEN: Fostering a Safe and Inclusive Community Culture

A community can have the most meticulously crafted guidelines, the most advanced moderation tools, and the most dedicated enforcement team, yet still feel unwelcoming, hostile, or toxic. This is because the health of a community is not merely defined by the absence of rule-breaking behavior. A truly thriving online space is defined by the presence of a positive culture—an environment where members feel not only protected from harm but also actively included, respected, and empowered to be their authentic selves. Fostering this culture is one of the most advanced and essential functions of a moderation team. It is the subtle, proactive work of shifting the community's focus from "what is not allowed" to "what we aspire to be."

Safety is the non-negotiable bedrock upon which this culture is built. It is the foundational layer of the community's hierarchy of needs. Before a member can feel a sense of belonging or self-expression, they must first feel safe from harassment, threats, and abuse. While reactive moderation is the primary tool for removing immediate threats, the *feeling* of safety is a cultural outcome. It is generated by the community's collective trust that the space is being managed fairly and competently. This trust is not built overnight; it is the cumulative result of thousands of consistent and transparent moderation actions.

The cornerstone of this feeling is the concept of **psychological safety**. This is a shared belief held by the members of a group that it is safe to take interpersonal risks. In an online community, this means a member feels they can ask a question that might seem basic without being mocked as a "newbie." It means they can propose an unconventional idea without being dogpiled for challenging the status quo. It means they can admit they made a mistake or don't know something without it being used as a weapon against them. When psychological safety is high, engagement flourishes. People are more willing to be vulnerable, to share their knowledge, and to participate in constructive debate.

A lack of psychological safety, by contrast, creates a culture of fear. Members become lurkers, afraid to post for fear of saying the wrong thing and inviting ridicule or attack. Conversations become dominated by a few loud, aggressive voices, and the diversity of thought that makes a community vibrant withers away. The primary way moderators build psychological safety is through the consistent and impartial enforcement of the guidelines. When members see that the rules against personal attacks apply just as rigorously to a popular, long-standing member as they do to a newcomer, it sends a powerful message that the space is governed by principle, not by personality or social cliques. Every time a moderator steps in to stop a user from being shamed for asking a simple question, they are making a deposit into the community's bank of psychological safety.

Safety, however, is merely the starting point. A space can be safe but still feel exclusionary. The next level of cultural development is **inclusion**. An inclusive community is one where people from all backgrounds and identities feel that they are welcomed, that their perspectives are valued, and that they have an equal opportunity to participate. It is about moving beyond a passive state of "we don't tolerate hate speech" to an active state of "we celebrate and support our diverse members." This is a significant shift in mindset that requires a proactive and often courageous approach from the moderation team.

This proactive stance means recognizing that harm is not limited to overt slurs and threats. The online environment is rife with **microaggressions**: the subtle, everyday comments, questions, and actions that communicate hostile, derogatory, or negative messages to individuals from marginalized groups. These are often unintentional, born of ignorance rather than malice, which makes them particularly challenging to moderate. A user might make a comment like, "You're so articulate," to a member of a racial minority, not intending it as an insult, but the underlying, condescending subtext is that they are surprised this person can speak well. Another might dismiss a female member's technical expertise with a "mansplaining" comment that they would not direct at a male peer.

Individually, a single microaggression may seem like a minor issue, a "gray area" not worth the trouble of addressing. This perspective fails to recognize the cumulative impact. For the person on the receiving end, it is not a single, isolated comment. It is one of a thousand tiny cuts they experience regularly. A community that permits a constant stream of these microaggressions is sending a clear signal to members of that group: "You are not truly welcome here. You are an outsider, and you must tolerate being treated as such."

Moderating microaggressions requires a different toolkit than moderating clear-cut rule violations. A heavy-handed, punitive response like a temporary suspension is often counterproductive, as the user who made the comment genuinely may not understand what they did wrong. The more effective approach is educational. A moderator can intervene with a gentle, public correction that focuses on the impact of the words, not the intent of the speaker. A comment like, "Hey, just a heads-up, the term 'spirit animal' has a specific cultural significance, so we try to avoid using it casually here," educates the user and the wider community without public shaming. A private message can be even more effective, explaining the issue in a non-confrontational way and providing the user with an opportunity to learn and adjust their behavior.

This proactive work extends to the language the community uses. An inclusive culture is mindful of its words. This means encouraging the use of gender-neutral language where appropriate ("Hey everyone," or "Hey folks," instead of "Hey guys"). It means respecting individuals' stated pronouns and having a clear policy of correcting those who refuse to do so. It means being conscious of and avoiding ableist language, such as using terms like "crazy" or "lame" as generic pejoratives. The moderators must be the primary models for this behavior. Their own communication sets the standard. When a moderator uses inclusive language consistently, it normalizes it for the entire community.

Representation is another powerful driver of inclusion. People are more likely to feel they belong when they see themselves reflected in the community. Moderators can actively foster this by amplifying the voices of a diverse range of members. This could mean featuring a insightful post by a newer member, highlighting a project created by someone from an underrepresented background, or ensuring that community events and discussions are relevant to a global, rather than a culturally specific, audience. If the community has a leadership team, ensuring that team is itself diverse sends the most powerful message of all.

Creating an inclusive culture also means being prepared to thoughtfully moderate difficult conversations about real-world social and political issues. The default instinct for many community managers is to ban such topics entirely to avoid the inevitable conflict. While this may be the right choice for some brand or product-focused communities, for many others, it is an abdication of responsibility that can make the community feel sterile and out of touch with reality. A blanket ban on "politics" can also be a form of covert exclusion, as what is considered "political" to a dominant group is often a matter of lived experience and identity for a marginalized one.

A more inclusive approach is to create a framework for these difficult conversations to occur respectfully. This can involve creating a dedicated, clearly marked channel or sub-forum for sensitive topics. Within that space, the moderation can be heavier and the rules of engagement more explicit. A pinned post might lay out the ground rules: "In this section, we demand a higher standard of discourse. All claims must be backed by evidence, there is zero tolerance for personal attacks, and the focus must remain on the respectful exchange of ideas." This strategy contains the conflict, provides a necessary outlet for important discussions, and demonstrates a commitment to free expression without allowing it to poison the rest of the community.

The practical work of fostering this culture begins on day one of a member's journey. The onboarding process is a critical opportunity to set expectations. The welcome message or pinned "Start Here" thread should not only link to the guidelines but also articulate the community's cultural values. A statement like, "We are a global community of people from all walks of life. We are committed to maintaining a welcoming environment for everyone, and we expect all our members to help us achieve that goal," explicitly frames the community as an inclusive space from the very beginning.

Accessibility is another practical expression of an inclusive culture. In a visual community, encouraging and modeling the use of descriptive "alt text" for images ensures that visually impaired members can participate. If the community shares video or audio content, providing transcripts or closed captions makes that content accessible to the hearing impaired. These are not just technical features; they are powerful signals that the community is actively working to include, rather than exclude, its members.

Building this culture also requires open and safe channels for feedback. Members need to feel that they can report not just clear rule violations but also these subtler cultural issues without fear of reprisal. They need a way to communicate with the moderation team if they feel a policy is having an exclusionary effect or if a moderator's action made them feel unsafe. This could be a private contact form, a dedicated feedback channel, or regular "town hall" style discussions where the leadership team actively solicits input from the community. A leadership team that listens, acknowledges mistakes, and demonstrates a willingness to evolve is a team that earns the trust necessary to guide a community's culture.

The work of building a safe and inclusive culture is a continuous process, not a destination. It is a constant series of small, deliberate actions: the gentle correction of a microaggression, the amplification of a new voice, the thoughtful reframing of a heated debate, the welcoming of a newcomer. These actions, when performed consistently by a dedicated moderation team, have a compounding effect. They build a powerful social norm, a cultural immune system where members themselves begin to model inclusive behavior, welcome newcomers, and marginalize those who seek to create a hostile environment. This is the ultimate goal:

to create a community that is not just free of bad behavior, but is fundamentally defined by its positive and welcoming character.

CHAPTER SIXTEEN: Empowering Community Members for Self-Moderation

A moderation team cannot be everywhere at once. As a community grows from a small town into a bustling city, the sheer volume of activity will inevitably outstrip the capacity of any centralized group of guardians. At this point, the long-term health and scalability of the community depend on a crucial cultural shift: the transition from a top-down model of enforcement to a collaborative model of shared responsibility. This is the principle of self-moderation, where the community itself becomes an active participant in maintaining its own health. This is not about the moderation team abdicating its duties; rather, it is the ultimate sign of their success. It signifies that the community's values have been so effectively established that the members themselves have become their most passionate defenders. The goal is to cultivate a powerful and resilient cultural immune system, where the community can naturally identify and contain disruptions, freeing the official moderators to focus on the most severe threats and the highest-level strategic work.

This empowerment does not happen overnight, and it is not an all-or-nothing proposition. It is a gradual process that can be thought of as a spectrum of increasing user involvement. At one end lies the most fundamental act of participation: reporting. In the middle are the informal systems of peer support and the creation of formalized "super user" roles. At the far end are platforms that build distributed moderation tools directly into the user experience, giving the community the power to collectively influence content visibility. Guiding a community along this spectrum requires a deliberate strategy of building trust, providing the right tools, and carefully managing the risks that come with distributing authority.

The foundation of all self-moderation is a simple, robust, and reliable reporting system. The "Report" button is the single most important tool you can give your community. It is the silent alarm that transforms every passive reader into a potential sentinel. As we have discussed, a moderation team cannot read every post, but the community as a whole can. By providing a clear and accessible reporting function on every piece of user-generated content, you create a force multiplier, leveraging the eyes of your entire user base. The effectiveness of this system, however, hinges on the user's confidence that their action will matter.

To foster this confidence, the reporting process cannot be a black box. When a user takes the time to file a report, they are making a small investment in the community's well-being. If they never hear anything back, if they see the content they reported remain visible for days, or if they have a consistently negative experience, they will simply stop trying. This is why providing feedback is so critical. While you should not share the specific disciplinary details of another user's case, a simple, automated notification—"Thank you for your report. We have reviewed the content and taken appropriate action"—is immensely powerful. It closes the loop, validates the user's effort, and confirms that the system is working. This simple act of acknowledgment is the fuel that keeps the engine of community reporting running.

As a community matures, a more organic and informal layer of self-moderation will begin to emerge. This is the domain of **peer correction**. You will start to see veteran members, without any official prompting, stepping in to perform the gentle maintenance work that keeps the community running smoothly. They are the ones who welcome a newcomer in an introductions thread, who patiently answer a frequently asked question for the tenth time, or who post a gentle reminder like, "Hey, let's keep this thread focused on the topic," when a conversation starts to stray. These members are not acting as enforcers; they are acting as helpful guides, embodying the community's culture and teaching its norms through their own positive example.

This behavior, while natural, can be actively cultivated by the official moderation team. The most powerful tool for this is positive reinforcement. When you see a member provide a particularly helpful answer or skillfully de-escalate a minor disagreement, take a moment to thank them publicly. A simple, "That's a fantastic explanation, @UserX, thanks for helping out!" does two things. First, it gives that user a small but meaningful dose of social recognition, rewarding their positive contribution. Second, it signals to the entire community that this type of helpful, supportive behavior is highly valued. Over time, this public praise helps to establish helpfulness as a high-status activity, creating a virtuous cycle where more members are motivated to participate in this informal stewardship.

For communities that wish to formalize this dynamic, the next step is to create a "Super User" or "Community Helper" program. This establishes a recognized, intermediate tier between the general user base and the official moderation team. These are not volunteer moderators with disciplinary powers. Instead, they are trusted, long-standing members who are granted a limited set of tools and a formal mandate to help nurture the community. The goal is to empower your most dedicated members to be even more effective in the helpful roles they are already playing.

The key to a successful super user program is a clearly defined, and intentionally limited, scope of responsibility. Their role is to help, not to punish. You would not grant them the ability to suspend or ban users. Instead, you would give them tools that amplify their helpfulness. This might include the ability to mark a question in a support forum as "Solved," the power to edit a post title for clarity, or the permission to tag and categorize content to improve its discoverability. A common and highly effective tool is to grant them a "priority flag," where any content they report is automatically pushed to the top of the official moderation queue for immediate review. This leverages their expert judgment to help the moderation team triage more efficiently.

Recruiting for such a program follows the same principles as recruiting for moderators. You look for the members who are already demonstrating the desired qualities: a history of helpfulness, a calm and patient temperament, and a deep understanding of the community's culture. The selection process itself is a form of recognition, and the "payment" for their service is typically status and access. They might be given a special badge or flair next to their username, a public acknowledgment of their trusted position. They should also be given a private communication channel with the moderation team, a space where they can ask for guidance, report trends they are seeing, and feel like valued insiders and true partners in the community's success.

At the far end of the empowerment spectrum are platforms that incorporate **distributed moderation tools** directly into the core user experience. These systems give the entire community a direct, albeit limited, role in shaping the visibility of content. The most common example of this is the upvote and downvote system, famously used by platforms like Reddit. In this model, the community's collective votes directly determine which content rises to the top and which is hidden from view. This is a powerful form of democratic, real-time content curation. A helpful comment is upvoted and becomes more visible; a rude or off-topic comment is downvoted into obscurity.

However, this model is not without its flaws. A voting system can easily create an echo chamber, where unpopular but perfectly valid opinions are consistently downvoted and suppressed. This is sometimes called the "heckler's veto," where the majority can effectively silence the minority simply by mass-downvoting their content. It also does not solve the problem of content that is popular but still violates the rules. A witty but hateful meme might get thousands of upvotes before the moderation team can intervene. Therefore, these systems must always be paired with a traditional reporting and moderation system to handle the rule violations that the court of public opinion might miss or even reward.

Another form of distributed moderation involves user-driven flagging systems. Some platforms can be configured to automatically take a limited action on a piece of content once it has been reported by a certain number of unique users. For example, a post that is flagged as spam by five different members might be automatically hidden from public view and placed in the moderation queue for a final decision. This can be an incredibly fast way to react to obvious spam waves or egregious rule violations, containing the damage before a human moderator is even alerted. The risk, of course, is that this system can be abused by coordinated groups or "brigades" who can mass-flag a user they disagree with in an attempt to get their content automatically hidden. The thresholds for these automated actions must be set and tuned with great care to balance the need for speed against the risk of abuse.

As with any distribution of power, empowering the community is not without its risks. The most common pitfall is the rise of **vigilantism**. If not properly guided, a group of empowered "super users" can sometimes develop into an exclusionary clique of "mini-mods" who are overly aggressive, pedantic, or hostile to newcomers. They might start to enforce their own personal interpretations of the rules or create an unwelcoming environment for anyone who challenges their authority. The official moderation team must be the ultimate source of truth and authority, and they must be prepared to step in and correct overzealous helpers. It must be made clear that the role of a super user is to be a guide, not a guard.

The risk of **burnout** is also a significant concern. Volunteers, even the most passionate ones, can become exhausted if they feel that the full weight of the community's health rests on their shoulders. It is crucial to manage expectations and to consistently reinforce that their role is to assist, not to replace, the official moderation team. Regular check-ins, expressions of gratitude, and a culture that encourages them to take breaks are all essential for the long-term sustainability of any volunteer helper program.

Finally, a moderator's role in a community with a strong culture of self-moderation undergoes a significant and positive evolution. They are no longer just the digital janitors, rushing from one mess to the next. The community itself is now handling a large portion of the routine cleanup. This frees the moderator to graduate from being a purely reactive firefighter to being a more strategic community architect. Their time is reallocated to higher-value activities: managing and mentoring the super user program, investigating the most complex and sensitive escalations, analyzing data to identify long-term community health trends, and developing the engagement initiatives that will help the community grow and thrive. Empowering the community is the final step in creating a truly scalable and resilient moderation strategy, one where the role of the moderator is not to be the sole source of control, but to be the catalyst for the community's own collective strength.

CHAPTER SEVENTEEN: Managing User-Generated Content Campaigns

A healthy community is in a constant state of creation, producing a steady, organic flow of user-generated content, or UGC. The moderation of this daily stream is the essential work of community maintenance. There are times, however, when an organization wishes to transform this gentle stream into a focused and powerful river. This is the purpose of a user-generated content campaign: a specific, time-bound initiative designed to encourage the community to create and submit content around a particular theme, often in exchange for a prize, recognition, or a chance to be featured. These campaigns are powerful marketing and engagement tools, but they also represent a unique and intense challenge for the moderation team.

Unlike the predictable rhythms of daily moderation, a UGC campaign is a planned event, a sprint rather than a marathon. The goal shifts from simply maintaining a safe environment to actively soliciting, collecting, and curating a high volume of content that meets specific criteria. This might be a photo contest asking customers to share pictures of themselves using a new product, a video competition for the most creative short film, or a call for written testimonials to be used in future advertising. While the principles of good moderation still apply, the context is fundamentally different. The stakes are often higher, the volume is concentrated, and the potential for both spectacular success and public relations disaster is magnified. Managing a campaign requires a shift in mindset from that of a community guardian to that of an event manager, a logistical expert, and a brand protector, all at once.

The success or failure of a UGC campaign is almost always determined long before the first submission is received. The planning phase is paramount, as it is here that the framework for an orderly, fair, and legally sound process is built. The first step is to establish a crystal-clear objective. What, precisely, is the campaign trying to achieve? Is the goal to gather authentic images for a new ad campaign? Is it to generate social media buzz and increase brand awareness? Is it to collect valuable product feedback from real users? A specific, measurable goal—such as "collect one thousand high-quality, approved photos of our product in use"—informs every subsequent decision, from the rules of the campaign to the resources allocated for moderation.

With a goal in place, the next task is to draft the campaign's rules and guidelines. This is a specialized and more stringent version of the community's general guidelines. Vague rules are an invitation to chaos, conflict, and user frustration. The campaign rules must be ruthlessly specific. What is the exact format for submissions? Are there size or length restrictions? What is the deadline, and in what time zone? Most importantly, what are the specific content requirements? If it is a photo contest for a beverage brand, the rules might need to state that the product's label must be clearly visible and that no competitor products can be present in the image. Every potential ambiguity must be identified and eliminated.

This is also the point where the legal team must be heavily involved. The question of content ownership and usage rights is the single greatest legal risk in a UGC campaign. The average user does not instinctively understand intellectual property law. They may not realize that submitting a photo gives the company the right to use it in a global advertising campaign. The terms and conditions of the campaign must spell this out in language that is both legally robust and easy for a layperson to understand. A standard approach is to require the user to affirm that they are the original creator of the content and to grant the company a broad, non-exclusive, worldwide, royalty-free license to use, reproduce, and display their submission in connection with the campaign and for future marketing purposes. This consent is the legal foundation of the entire endeavor.

Once the rules are set, the moderation team must begin its own logistical planning. A successful campaign will generate a sudden and massive spike in content volume, and the daily moderation schedule will almost certainly be insufficient. The first step is to forecast the expected number of submissions. Based on this forecast, the team must create a moderation staffing plan. Will the current team need to work overtime? Do additional moderators need to be trained and brought on board on a temporary basis? Can you schedule moderators in shifts to ensure the submission queue is being monitored consistently, especially around the campaign's launch and deadline? Waiting until the campaign is live to discover you are understaffed is a recipe for a massive backlog and a poor user experience.

The moderation workflow itself must also be designed and configured. Will submissions be collected through a hashtag on a social media platform, or will they be funneled through a dedicated upload portal on a website? A dedicated portal offers far more control, allowing you to force users to check a box agreeing to the terms and conditions before they can even upload their content. The moderation queue for the campaign should be separate from the general community queue, allowing the team to focus its efforts. This is also the time to prepare any automated tools. If the campaign requires a certain logo to be present in an image, a computer vision AI can be trained to perform a first-pass check, immediately flagging submissions that fail this basic requirement.

With the plan in place, the campaign goes live, and the focus shifts to execution. The single most important strategic decision for a live campaign is the choice between pre-moderation and post-moderation. In a pre-moderation model, every single submission is held in a private queue and must be manually approved by a moderator before it becomes visible to the public. The primary advantage of this approach is safety. It gives the brand absolute control over what appears on its campaign page, virtually eliminating the risk of offensive, off-topic, or brand-damaging content being publicly associated with the campaign. The downside is that it is slow. The delay between submission and publication can stifle the sense of real-time community engagement and excitement.

Post-moderation is the opposite. Submissions go live instantly, appearing on the public-facing gallery or feed as soon as the user hits "submit." The moderation team then reviews this live content and retroactively removes anything that violates the rules. This approach fosters a much more dynamic and immediate user experience, encouraging participation and a sense of shared, real-time activity. The risk, of course, is significant. A single, highly offensive submission can be seen by thousands of people before a moderator has a chance to remove it, and a screenshot of that content can live on forever. The choice between these two models depends on the brand's tolerance for risk, the nature of its audience, and the resources available for rapid-response moderation. For most brand-sensitive contests, a pre-moderation approach is the safer and more prudent choice.

Regardless of the model chosen, the moderation team will spend the duration of the campaign living in the triage queue. Their workflow must be efficient and consistent. A typical submission will be sorted into one of three buckets: Approved, Rejected, or Escalate. "Approved" means the content meets all the campaign rules and is cleared for publication. "Rejected" means it clearly violates a rule and is discarded. "Escalate" is for the gray-area cases that require a second opinion from a senior moderator or a legal consultation.

Consistency is the bedrock of a fair campaign. A team of moderators must be calibrated to interpret the rules in the same way. One moderator cannot be approving submissions with blurry logos while another is rejecting them for the same reason. This is where the internal moderator handbook becomes critical, with a specific section dedicated to the campaign's rules and examples of what constitutes an acceptable or unacceptable submission. Regular check-ins with the moderation team throughout the campaign are essential to ensure everyone remains aligned.

During the campaign, the team will face a predictable set of challenges. The most common issue will be an avalanche of well-intentioned but ineligible submissions. These are the users who failed to read the rules carefully. They might submit a photo that doesn't feature the product, a video that is too long, or an entry that is completely off-topic. The key here is to have a set of pre-written, templated rejection messages that are polite and clear. A simple, "Thank you for your submission! Unfortunately, we were not able to approve your entry as it did not meet the requirement of featuring our product. We encourage you to review the rules and try again," is far better than a silent rejection.

The team must also be vigilant for fraud. If the campaign involves a voting component, some users will inevitably try to game the system. They may create dozens of fake accounts to vote for their own entry, or use automated scripts to inflate their score. Moderators must use their tools to look for suspicious patterns, such as a sudden surge of votes from newly created accounts with no other activity or a large number of votes coming from the same IP address. Similarly, submissions must be vetted for originality. A quick reverse-image search can often reveal if a stunning photograph submitted to the contest was, in fact, stolen from a professional photographer's website.

Perhaps the most dangerous threat is campaign hijacking, sometimes known as "hashtag bombing." This occurs when a person or group, often for political or activist reasons, decides to co-opt the campaign's platform for their own message. They can flood a campaign hashtag with negative or offensive content, turning a positive marketing effort into a public relations crisis. This is a form of a small-scale crisis. The response must be swift and coordinated. The moderation team must go into high alert, rapidly removing the offending content while the community management or PR team decides on a public-facing response. This is a prime example of why post-moderation can be so risky for high-profile campaigns.

Once the submission deadline passes, the work is not yet over. The post-campaign phase is about closing out the event in a way that leaves the community feeling positive and respected. The first and most enjoyable task is to announce and celebrate the winners. This is the payoff for all the hard work, a chance to showcase the best and most creative content the community has produced. This act of celebration reinforces the value of participation and encourages members to join in future events.

After the winners are announced, the team must be prepared to handle the inevitable flood of inquiries from participants whose entries were not selected or were rejected. Diplomacy and transparency are crucial. The moderator's response should be polite, professional, and should always refer back to the specific, objective rules of the campaign. Having a clear, well-written set of rules is the best possible defense against accusations of unfairness.

Finally, the team must engage in a thorough post-mortem. This involves analyzing the campaign's data and measuring it against the initial goals. How many total submissions were received? What was the final approval rate? Which rules caused the most confusion for users, leading to the highest number of rejections? How many moderator hours did the campaign consume? This data is invaluable for planning future campaigns, allowing the team to refine its rules, improve its workflow, and make more accurate resource forecasts. The collected UGC must also be properly managed. All the approved content needs to be archived and tagged in a central repository, ensuring that the marketing team can easily find and use this valuable asset in the future, always in accordance with the rights the users have granted. From start to finish, a UGC campaign is a microcosm of the entire moderation discipline, requiring careful planning, precise execution, and a deep respect for both the brand's reputation and the community's creative spirit.

CHAPTER EIGHTEEN: Scaling Moderation for Growing Communities

There are few problems more desirable for a community manager than the one posed by rapid, explosive growth. What was once a quiet, intimate gathering of a few hundred dedicated members has, through some combination of luck and good management, become a bustling metropolis of thousands, or even millions. The forums are buzzing, the content is flowing, and the energy is palpable. This is the dream. It is also a logistical nightmare waiting to happen. The ad-hoc, personal, and often heroic moderation efforts that sustained the community in its youth are the first things to buckle and break under the immense pressure of scale. The moderation queue, once a manageable inbox, becomes an overflowing, Sisyphean torrent. Response times stretch from minutes to days. The delicate cultural balance begins to fray.

Scaling moderation is not simply about doing more of the same, nor is it just about hiring more people. Adding more moderators to a broken system will only create a more expensive and chaotic broken system. True scaling is a strategic evolution. It is a deliberate transition from an artisanal craft to an industrial process, a shift from relying on individual judgment to relying on robust, documented systems. It requires a fundamental rethinking of team structures, a deeper and more strategic integration of technology, and a disciplined, data-driven approach to management. This chapter is about navigating that transition, ensuring that the very success that makes your community great does not become the cause of its eventual collapse.

The first casualty of scale is the informal process. In a small community, the moderation team, which may be just one person, operates on a deep, instinctual understanding of the members and the culture. They know who the regulars are, they can read the subtext of conversations, and they can often resolve disputes with a quick, personalized message. This "gut-feel" moderation is highly effective but utterly unscalable. When the community has a million members, you can no longer know everyone. You cannot rely on personal history to contextualize a user's behavior. A decision that seems obvious and fair to one moderator can seem arbitrary and biased to another who lacks the same context. This inconsistency is poison to a large community, eroding the trust that is the foundation of perceived fairness.

The antidote to this chaos is formalization. Every process that was once an unspoken understanding must be meticulously documented and standardized. The internal Moderator Handbook, discussed in an earlier chapter, transforms from a helpful guide into the single source of truth for the entire operation. It must evolve into a comprehensive operational manual, detailing not just the "what" of the guidelines but the "how" of their enforcement. It should contain a library of common edge cases and the official precedent for how they are to be handled. This document ensures that a moderator in Dublin and a moderator in Manila, working twelve hours apart on the same queue, will arrive at the same conclusion when faced with the same violation.

This standardization must extend to communication. At scale, the luxury of crafting a unique, personal message for every warning or content removal disappears. The team must develop a suite of pre-written, templated responses for the most common infractions. This is not about being impersonal; it is about being consistent, clear, and efficient. A good template is a model of clarity. It states the specific content that was actioned, quotes the specific rule that was violated, provides a link to the full guidelines for review, and outlines the next step in the escalation ladder. Using these templates ensures that every user receives the same professional, non-confrontational message, which depersonalizes the enforcement and reduces the likelihood of a protracted argument.

A formalized escalation path is equally critical. In a small team, a difficult case might be debated in a group chat until a consensus is reached. At scale, this is a bottleneck that grinds the entire system to a halt. A clear, multi-tiered triage and escalation system is required. The policy must explicitly define who is empowered to make what decisions. A frontline moderator should be able to

117

handle a simple spam post on their own, but a credible threat of violence or a complex legal complaint must be immediately escalated to a specialized team or a senior leader without debate. This ensures that the team's most experienced and highly-trained members are dedicating their time to the most complex and high-risk issues, rather than getting bogged down in the daily deluge.

As the processes are formalized, the structure of the team itself must evolve. A flat hierarchy where every moderator does a little bit of everything is inefficient at scale. The solution is to move toward a tiered and specialized model, mirroring the structure of other large-scale operational teams like customer support or network operations. A tiered moderation structure creates a clear flow of work and a career path for team members.

At the base is Tier 1, the frontline moderators. This group is responsible for handling the highest volume of content, focusing on the least complex issues. They are the masters of the main moderation queue, rapidly clearing out the obvious spam, the unambiguous profanity, and the clear-cut violations that make up the bulk of reported content. Because their work is highly procedural and guided by the detailed handbook, this tier can be staffed by newer moderators, part-time staff, or, for many global platforms, by a dedicated team from a Business Process Outsourcing (BPO) partner.

Tier 2 is composed of senior or specialist moderators. They handle the escalations from Tier 1. These are the gray-area cases that require deep contextual understanding, the heated disputes between long-standing members, and the initial review of sensitive or graphic content. These moderators are typically veterans of the community with proven judgment and excellent communication skills. They act as a crucial filter, resolving the majority of complex issues before they need to be escalated further.

At the top is Tier 3, which is often a small group of Trust & Safety professionals, policy leads, or the Community Manager. This tier handles the most critical and highest-risk escalations: credible threats requiring contact with law enforcement, formal legal takedown notices, reports of child safety issues, and the final review of user appeals. This group is also responsible for analyzing the trends reported by the lower tiers to identify gaps in policy, emerging threats, and the need for new moderation tools or training.

Alongside this tiered structure, specialization becomes a necessity. A single moderator cannot be an expert in everything from copyright law to regional political conflicts. As a platform grows, it will need to develop dedicated teams or individuals who focus on specific, high-harm problem areas. A Hate Speech team will receive specialized training on coded language, hateful symbols, and the ideologies of extremist groups. A Misinformation team might be composed of individuals with strong analytical and research skills who are trained to vet factual claims. A live-stream moderation team will be trained to operate in a high-pressure, real-time environment. This specialization ensures that the most difficult content is being handled by the people best equipped to understand its nuance.

This scaled human workforce must be augmented by a new generation of technological tools. The role of automation and AI at scale is not just to catch bad content, but to fundamentally reduce the cognitive load on the human moderators. The goal is to ensure that a human's valuable and limited attention is spent only on the content that truly requires human judgment. This begins with the moderation dashboard itself. A simple list of reported posts is no longer sufficient. A scaled platform needs a sophisticated queueing system that functions like an enterprise-grade ticketing platform, with features for assigning cases, tracking their status, and logging every action taken for auditing purposes.

AI is the engine of this load reduction. In a scaled system, AI models are used not only to flag potentially violating content but also to proactively clear obviously safe content. If a model is 99.9% confident that a post from a user with a pristine reputation is benign, that post can be allowed to bypass the moderation queue entirely. Conversely, the system can be configured to take automatic action on violations where the confidence score is extremely high. A known spam bot or a confirmed CSAM hash does not require a human review; it requires immediate, automated removal and reporting.

The most advanced scaled systems use technology to move from a reactive to a proactive posture. Instead of waiting for users to report a problem, the system actively hunts for it. AI can be trained to detect the statistical anomalies that signal a coordinated attack, such as a sudden spike in new accounts all using similar language in the same thread. It can identify the early signs of a brigading attempt by monitoring for unnatural voting patterns. This proactive threat detection allows the moderation team to get ahead of a crisis, locking down threads or deploying other countermeasures before a situation can spiral out of control. Workflow automation is the final piece of the technological puzzle, with the system intelligently routing reports to the appropriate specialized team—a copyright claim goes to the legal queue, a harassment report goes to the Trust & Safety queue—without any manual triage required.

For many global platforms, the only economically viable way to achieve 24/7 human moderation coverage is through Business Process Outsourcing (BPO). By partnering with firms that have large moderation teams in different time zones, a platform can create a "follow-the-sun" model, ensuring that the moderation queue is being actively worked on at every hour of the day. This provides immense benefits in terms of cost and speed. However, it also introduces significant risks that must be carefully managed. The greatest challenge is maintaining quality and cultural attunement. An outsourced moderator in a different country may not grasp the subtle, unwritten social norms of your community, leading to culturally deaf decisions that can alienate your user base.

Successful BPO partnerships require a massive investment in documentation and communication. The Moderator Handbook becomes the bible, and a rigorous "train-the-trainer" program is essential to ensure the policies are understood correctly. A dedicated, in-house vendor manager must act as a constant bridge between the company's policy team and the outsourced workforce.

Most importantly, a strict and continuous Quality Assurance (QA) program must be in place. This involves the in-house team regularly auditing a sample of the BPO's decisions to measure accuracy, provide feedback, and identify areas where additional training is needed. The ethical considerations are also paramount; a platform is responsible for ensuring that its outsourcing partners provide adequate psychological support and a healthy working environment for the moderators who are often reviewing the most disturbing content on its behalf.

Finally, a scaled moderation system cannot fly blind. It must be guided by data. Relying on anecdotal evidence or the "loudest" complaints is a recipe for biased and ineffective policy. A data-driven approach allows you to understand the true health of your community and the efficiency of your operations in an objective way. The team must track a core set of key performance indicators. Queue Volume tells you how much content is being flagged and helps with staffing forecasts. Time to Action, the average time it takes to handle a report, is a direct measure of your team's responsiveness. Moderator Accuracy, measured through QA audits, tells you how consistently your policies are being applied.

More advanced metrics provide a higher-level view of the community's health. The Appeal Rate, the percentage of moderation decisions that users formally appeal, can be an early warning sign of an unclear policy or a poorly performing moderator. The ultimate goal for many large platforms is to reduce the Prevalence of Violating Content (VVC), which is the measure of what percentage of content views are of material that breaks the rules. Lowering this number is a direct indication that the entire scaled system—from proactive AI filters to the human review teams—is successfully reducing the amount of harm that users are exposed to. This data is the feedback loop that drives the entire scaling process. It tells you when you need to hire more people, where you need to improve your training, and which of your technological tools are providing the greatest return on investment. Scaling is not a one-time project; it is a continuous cycle of formalizing, structuring, automating, and measuring, all in the service of preserving the community's culture, no matter how large it grows.

CHAPTER NINETEEN: Crisis Management: Handling Large-Scale Incidents

Every community has its bad days. There are days when a new spam bot slips through the filters, when a popular thread devolves into an unusually nasty flame war, or when a minor site feature breaks, causing a flood of user complaints. These are the routine fires, the predictable challenges that a well-trained moderation team is equipped to handle as part of its daily operational rhythm. A crisis, however, is a different beast entirely. A crisis is not a routine fire; it is a wildfire. It is a sudden, large-scale event that moves faster than normal processes can contain, threatening the fundamental stability, safety, or public reputation of the community. It is the moment when the standard operating procedures are no longer sufficient, and an emergency response is required.

A crisis can erupt from anywhere. It might be a technical vulnerability, such as a bug that allows users to post malicious code or bypass privacy settings, leading to widespread panic. It could be a social catastrophe, like a viral piece of dangerous misinformation or a "challenge" that spreads rapidly across the platform, encouraging harmful behavior. It might be a targeted attack, such as a coordinated, large-scale harassment campaign or "raid" organized by a hostile external group intent on shutting down your community. Or, it could be the digital fallout from a real-world tragedy, where a flood of grief, anger, and speculation overwhelms the community's capacity for civil discourse. These are the "black swan" events that can define a community's legacy, for better or for worse.

The single most important rule of crisis management is this: the worst possible time to create a crisis management plan is in the middle of a crisis. When the alarms are blaring and the community is in chaos, the pressure, confusion, and influx of information make clear, rational decision-making nearly impossible. Adrenaline and panic are poor substitutes for a well-rehearsed plan. A formal crisis management plan is the community's fire escape map. You hope you never have to use it, but you practice the drills and check the exits regularly, because when the smoke starts pouring in, there is no time to consult an architect. Preparation is the only thing that separates a controlled, effective response from a panicked, chaotic one.

The foundation of any good plan is the establishment of a dedicated Crisis Response Team. In the heat of the moment, you cannot be fumbling to figure out who needs to be in the room. This team should be a cross-functional group of designated individuals with clearly defined roles. This is not just a job for the moderation team. The core team typically includes a Crisis Commander—a senior leader, often the Head of Community or Trust & Safety, who has the ultimate authority to make decisions. It must also include leads from the moderation team, Public Relations or Communications, Legal, and the relevant Engineering or Product teams. Each person must know their specific responsibility: Legal assesses the liability, PR drafts the public statements, Engineering works on the technical fix, and the moderation lead directs the frontline containment efforts.

This core team needs a pre-established, secure communication channel—the digital "war room." This could be a dedicated, locked Slack channel, a persistent video conference bridge, or a group chat that can be activated at a moment's notice. This channel becomes the single source of truth for the duration of the crisis. It is where real-time information is shared, decisions are debated and made, and actions are coordinated. This prevents the fatal mistake of having fragmented conversations happening in different places, which leads to confusion and duplicated effort. The war room is the brain of the operation, processing information and sending clear signals to the rest of the body.

To avoid overreacting to minor issues or underreacting to major ones, the plan must include a clear Triage and Severity Framework. This framework defines different levels of crisis, each with its own pre-approved activation protocol. For example, a Level 3 incident might be a serious but contained issue, such as a harassment pile-on against a single user, which could be handled by the on-duty senior moderators. A Level 2 incident could be a major site disruption affecting a large portion of the user base, requiring the activation of the full Crisis Response Team during business hours. A Level 1 incident is the existential threat—a massive data breach, a viral threat of violence—that requires the immediate, 24/7 activation of the entire team, regardless of the time of day, and includes notifying executive leadership.

The final piece of preparation is the creation of a playbook. Just as an airline has a checklist for engine failure, a community should have a playbook for its most predictable crisis scenarios. You cannot anticipate every possible disaster, but you can plan for the most likely categories. A "Viral Misinformation Playbook" would have a checklist of initial steps: contact the subject matter expert team, deploy fact-checking labels, and use AI to identify and down-rank duplicates. A "Doxxing and Harassment Campaign Playbook" would include steps for immediately securing the victim's account, performing a mass removal of the offending content, and preserving evidence for law enforcement. These playbooks provide the crucial muscle memory that allows the team to act decisively in the chaotic opening moments of an incident.

When a crisis does strike, the first sixty minutes are often the most critical. This is the "golden hour" where the actions taken can dramatically alter the trajectory of the event. The response begins with Detection and Alerting. How does the organization know a crisis is unfolding? It might be a sudden, dramatic spike in user reports about a specific topic. It could be an automated monitoring tool that detects an unusual surge in account creations. Or it could be a message from the PR team who saw the community's name trending on Twitter for all the wrong reasons. The plan must include a reliable, 24/7 method for an on-duty moderator to immediately trigger an alert that assembles the core Crisis Response Team.

Once the team is assembled in the war room, the first priority is Situation Assessment. The team must work quickly to establish the ground truth. What do we know for certain? What is speculation? Who is impacted? What is the scope of the problem? This is a fact-finding mission, not a blame-finding one. The frontline moderators are the key intelligence source here, feeding real-time observations from the community directly into the war room. It is critical to get a clear picture of the facts before making any major decisions or public statements.

While the situation is being assessed, the immediate operational goal is Containment. The objective is to stop the bleeding and prevent the problem from spreading further. This is where the moderators on the front lines become the emergency first responders. Based on direction from the Crisis Commander, they will execute a series of immediate actions. This could involve locking down hundreds of inflammatory threads, temporarily putting the entire community into a "read-only" or "restricted" mode to stop the flow of new content, deploying a team to mass-ban accounts participating in a raid, or working with engineers to temporarily disable the feature that is being exploited. These are blunt, powerful tools, and their use is a clear sign that the situation has moved beyond normal moderation.

As the operational team works on containment, the communications team faces its own urgent task: managing the narrative. Silence is the enemy in a crisis. In the absence of information from the platform, the community will fill the void with its own speculation, rumors, and fear, which is almost always worse than the reality. The first public communication should happen as quickly as possible, even if you do not have all the answers. This initial message is a "holding statement." It is not a detailed explanation; it is an acknowledgment. A simple, "We are aware of the ongoing issue affecting [the community feature] and our team is actively investigating. We take this very seriously and will provide another update within the hour," achieves three critical goals. It shows you are aware, it shows you are working on it, and it sets a clear expectation for when more information will come.

Throughout the crisis, communication must be a steady, reliable drumbeat. Even if the update is, "We are still investigating and do not have new information at this time," it is better than silence. The moderator's role in this process is to be a unified front. They should be equipped with the approved public messaging and should use it consistently in any interactions with the community. They must resist the urge to speculate or to provide their own personal commentary on the situation. During a crisis, the team speaks with a single, calm, and authoritative voice.

The role of the individual moderator during a crisis is one of the most intense and stressful in the entire field. Their primary job is to execute the plan with speed and precision. They are the hands of the crisis team, carrying out the mass content removals and user sanctions that are necessary for containment. They must also act as a crucial feedback loop, funneling intelligence from the community back to the war room. They are the ones who will see the new tactics the attackers are using or the new rumors that are gaining traction among the user base. They must do all of this while maintaining a professional and composed public demeanor, knowing that the anxious community is watching their every move.

Once the immediate threat has been neutralized—the bug is patched, the raid has subsided, the misinformation has been contained—the crisis moves into its final phase: recovery. The first step is to communicate a resolution. When the incident is over, the community deserves a transparent and honest explanation. This is the time for the full post-mortem statement. This statement should explain what happened in clear, simple terms, take responsibility for the platform's role in the failure, detail the steps that were taken to resolve it, and, most importantly, outline the specific changes that will be made to prevent the same thing from happening again. This transparency is the painful but necessary price of rebuilding trust.

Internally, the Crisis Response Team must conduct its own blameless post-mortem. The goal of this meeting is not to find an individual to blame, but to dissect the process to find its weaknesses. What parts of our plan worked well? Where did our process break down? Was our playbook for this scenario adequate? Did we have the right people in the war room? The output of this meeting should be a concrete list of action items to improve the crisis management plan, ensuring the organization learns from the experience and becomes more resilient.

Finally, and most importantly, the leadership must turn its attention to the human cost of the crisis. The moderators and other staff who have just spent hours or days in a high-stress, high-stakes environment will be exhausted and emotionally drained. They have likely been exposed to a concentrated and overwhelming amount of toxic content and user anger. A post-crisis debrief is essential, not just to review the process, but to allow the team to decompress. Leaders must acknowledge the team's extraordinary effort, check in on their well-being, and ensure they have access to the time off and mental health resources needed to recover from the experience. A crisis can forge a team into a stronger, more cohesive unit, but only if its people are cared for once the smoke has cleared.

CHAPTER TWENTY: The Well-being of a Moderator: Dealing with Burnout and Trauma

The previous chapters have treated moderation as a series of processes, a collection of skills, and a strategic function. We have discussed the tools, the rules, and the tactics required to manage a community effectively. But behind every filtered word, every deleted comment, and every banned account is a human being. The moderator is the essential human element in the system, and that humanity comes at a cost. The work of an online community moderator is not merely a technical or administrative task; it is a profound act of emotional labor, carried out under conditions that can be psychologically taxing in the extreme. Moderators are the digital world's first responders, its sanitation workers, and its crisis counselors, all rolled into one. They are required to calmly and systematically engage with the very content that the rest of the community is being protected from.

This constant exposure to the best and, more often, the worst of human behavior takes a toll. Over time, the relentless pressure, the negativity, and the exposure to traumatic material can lead to serious psychological harm. This is the hidden occupational hazard of the profession. To build a sustainable, long-term moderation practice, an organization must treat the well-being of its moderators not as a soft perk or an afterthought, but as a core operational necessity. A moderation team that is burned out, traumatized, and unsupported is an ineffective one. This chapter will move beyond the mechanics of moderation and focus on the health of the mechanic, exploring the twin threats of burnout and vicarious trauma and outlining the strategies, both individual and organizational, that are essential for survival.

Burnout is a state of emotional, physical, and mental exhaustion caused by prolonged or excessive stress. In the context of moderation, it is far more than simply feeling tired after a long shift. It is a chronic condition characterized by three distinct symptoms. The first is overwhelming emotional exhaustion, a feeling of being completely drained and having nothing left to give. The second is depersonalization or cynicism, where the moderator develops a detached, callous, or excessively negative attitude toward their work and the community members they are meant to serve. The third is a diminished sense of personal accomplishment, a feeling that their work is futile and makes no real difference.

The drivers of moderator burnout are woven into the very fabric of the job. The sheer volume of work is often a primary factor. A moderator in a large community may be tasked with reviewing hundreds or even thousands of flagged items per day. The task can feel like trying to empty the ocean with a thimble—a repetitive, endless, and often thankless stream of negativity. Each item in that queue, no matter how trivial, requires a small act of judgment, and the cumulative effect of these thousands of micro-decisions leads to a specific kind of mental exhaustion known as decision fatigue. As the brain's capacity for rational decision-making becomes depleted, the quality of moderation suffers, and the risk of making inconsistent or poor choices increases.

Compounding this is the constant exposure to hostility. Moderators are the designated targets for community frustration. They are the public face of every unpopular decision, the recipients of an endless stream of criticism, personal insults, and accusations of bias. The role requires them to absorb this anger and respond with unwavering professionalism. This constant performance of emotional labor—suppressing one's own feelings of anger or hurt to project an image of calm neutrality—is incredibly draining. It is a form of psychological armor that is heavy to wear, day in and day out.

The nature of the work often fosters a sense of isolation. Many moderators work remotely, alone in a home office or at a kitchen table. They are physically disconnected from their teammates, and the confidential nature of their work means they cannot simply vent to a spouse or friend about the specifics of their day. They inhabit a strange world, deeply enmeshed in the social drama of a community yet separate from it. This can lead to a feeling of being a perpetual outsider, a ghost in the machine. When this is combined with the sense of futility that can arise from dealing with intractable problems like trolling, it creates a perfect storm for burnout.

The symptoms can manifest gradually. It might start with increased irritability or a shorter temper. The moderator may find themselves becoming overly sarcastic or cynical about the community members in private team channels. Their motivation plummets, and the work that once felt meaningful now feels like a chore. The quality of their work may decline, with an increase in mistakes or missed violations. In some cases, the stress can manifest physically, leading to headaches, stomach issues, or trouble sleeping. Recognizing these signs, both in oneself and in one's colleagues, is the first step toward addressing the problem before it becomes a crisis.

While burnout is a serious risk, it is arguably the lesser of the two great psychological threats a moderator faces. The second, and far more acute, danger is vicarious trauma, also known as secondary traumatic stress. This is a profound and often debilitating psychological injury that can occur from repeated exposure to the traumatic experiences of others. It is not the same as burnout. Burnout is the result of being overwhelmed by the stresses of the job; vicarious trauma is the result of absorbing the trauma of the content itself. It is the emotional and psychological residue that is left behind after viewing horrific material.

The moderators on the front lines of large platforms are routinely exposed to the darkest corners of the human experience. They are the ones who must view graphic and realistic depictions of violence, from accidents and war footage to acts of terrorism and murder. They are tasked with reviewing content related to self-harm and suicide, sometimes in real-time. They must read through the vilest forms of hate speech and the most detailed, threatening forms of harassment. And, in the most extreme cases, they are the ones who must identify and report Child Sexual Abuse Material

(CSAM), a task that is almost universally recognized as one of the most psychologically damaging jobs in the digital world.

This exposure is not like watching a horror movie. The content is real, and the victims are real. This reality can fundamentally alter a moderator's perception of the world. It can shatter their pre-existing beliefs about safety, trust, and the inherent goodness of people. They can begin to see potential threats everywhere, becoming hypervigilant and anxious in their daily lives. The world outside their screen can start to feel as dangerous and hostile as the world within it.

The symptoms of vicarious trauma mirror those of post-traumatic stress disorder (PTSD). A moderator may experience intrusive and unwanted thoughts or mental images of the content they have reviewed, long after they have logged off. They may have nightmares or flashbacks. They may feel a sense of emotional numbness and detachment from their loved ones, or they may become prone to sudden and uncharacteristic outbursts of anger. Many develop avoidance behaviors, actively trying to stay away from people, places, or even news stories that remind them of the content they have seen. It is a serious and persistent psychological injury, and it is a direct and foreseeable consequence of the work. It is crucial to understand that this is not a sign of personal weakness or a failure to cope; it is a normal human reaction to an abnormal and deeply traumatic experience.

Given these profound risks, the practice of self-care is not a luxury for a moderator; it is a fundamental survival skill. The responsibility for well-being is shared between the individual and the organization, and it begins with the strategies that a moderator can employ to protect themselves on a daily basis. The most important of these is the conscious and deliberate creation of boundaries. The line between work and life must be stark and well-defended, especially for remote moderators for whom the office is always just a few feet away.

This means establishing clear "log on" and "log off" times and sticking to them religiously. When the workday is over, it is over.

All work-related notifications on personal devices should be silenced. The temptation to just quickly check the queue one last time before bed must be resisted. For many remote workers, a "shutdown ritual" can be a powerful psychological tool. This could be as simple as closing the laptop, tidying the desk, and then immediately leaving the room to go for a short walk. This symbolic act helps to create the mental separation that a physical commute once provided, signaling to the brain that the work portion of the day is complete.

During the workday itself, moderators must practice active decompression. It is not healthy to spend eight consecutive hours immersed in a toxic moderation queue. Taking short, frequent breaks away from the screen is essential. This is not just a lunch break; it is a series of five- or ten-minute intervals to stand up, stretch, look out a window, or do a few deep breathing exercises. After a particularly difficult session, such as reviewing a piece of graphic content, it is vital to have a "palate cleanser." This involves intentionally engaging with something positive and life-affirming. It could be looking at pictures of a beloved pet, listening to a favorite song, or watching a short, funny video. This small act can help to break the hold of the negative material and prevent it from lingering in the mind.

Cognitive reframing is another powerful individual technique. This involves consciously changing the way one thinks about the job and the abuse that comes with it. A moderator must learn to develop a professional detachment, to constantly remind themselves that the anger and insults from users are not directed at them as a person. They are directed at a role, at a symbol of authority, at a username in a different color. The mantra "they are angry at the uniform, not at me" can be a powerful shield against internalizing the hostility. It is also helpful to focus on the purpose and the positive impact of the work. Every piece of spam removed, every harasser banned, and every piece of illegal content reported is a concrete action that makes the community safer for millions of other users. Holding onto this sense of purpose can be a powerful antidote to the feeling of futility.

The value of peer support cannot be overstated. The private, internal channel for the moderation team is more than just a place to discuss work; it is a vital support network. It is the one place where moderators can talk to other people who truly understand the unique pressures of the job. Sharing a difficult experience with a teammate, asking for a second opinion, or simply venting in a safe space can be incredibly therapeutic. This is also where the often-misunderstood phenomenon of "gallows humor" comes into play. Sharing dark jokes about the absurd or horrific content they see is a time-honored coping mechanism for first responders and others in high-trauma professions. In the privacy of a trusted team, this shared humor can be a way of processing the unthinkable and reaffirming a sense of shared reality.

While these individual strategies are essential, they are not enough. The ultimate responsibility for protecting the well-being of moderators rests with the organization that employs them. A company cannot simply hire people, expose them to traumatic material, and then place the entire burden of managing the psychological consequences on their shoulders. A responsible organization builds a comprehensive, multi-layered system of support that treats moderator wellness as a critical safety issue.

This system begins with the operational design of the work itself. One of the most effective strategies is the deliberate limitation of exposure. No single moderator should be assigned to review the most sensitive and graphic content queues (such as CSAM or graphic violence) for their entire shift, day after day. The work must be rotated. A moderator might spend one hour in the graphic content queue, followed by two hours in the general spam queue, and then an hour on non-queue-based project work. This rotation provides a built-in "palate cleanser" and prevents any one person from becoming saturated with the most damaging material.

Technology can also be designed to protect, not just to enable. Moderation tools can and should be built with psychological wellness features. For example, all potentially graphic or sensitive images and videos can be blurred or rendered in grayscale by default. The moderator would then have to make a conscious choice to click a button to view the content in its original form. This small act of friction returns a sense of control to the moderator. It is no longer a passive stream of horror being pushed at them; it is a controlled environment where they choose when and how to engage with the material. Audio from videos can be muted by default, and text-based tools can be used to flag particularly vile language, giving the moderator a warning before they read a comment.

Training and education are another pillar of organizational support. The onboarding process for a new moderator must include a mandatory and comprehensive module on the psychological risks of the job. They must be taught the signs and symptoms of burnout and vicarious trauma, both in themselves and in their teammates. They should be equipped with a starter kit of resilience techniques and coping strategies from day one. This knowledge normalizes the experience; it reassures the moderator that their psychological reactions are not a sign of failure, but a predictable consequence of the work, and that there are established methods for managing them.

The most critical component of any organizational wellness program is providing access to professional mental health support. This is non-negotiable. The company must provide and pay for confidential access to therapists and counselors, and these professionals should ideally be trained specifically in dealing with trauma. This cannot be a reactive system where a moderator has to ask for help after they are already in crisis. The support should be proactive. This can take the form of mandatory, regular wellness check-ins, where a moderator has a scheduled, paid session with a counselor simply to talk about how they are doing. This destigmatizes the act of seeking help and builds a preventative, rather than a purely remedial, system of care.

Finally, the culture of the team and the behavior of its managers are the glue that holds all of these initiatives together. Managers of moderation teams need their own specialized training. They must be taught how to spot the early warning signs of distress in their team members and how to initiate a supportive, non-judgmental conversation. They must foster a culture of psychological safety within the team, where a moderator feels safe to raise their hand and say, "I've hit my limit for the day," without fearing that it will be seen as a sign of weakness or that it will negatively impact their career. The leadership must constantly and publicly acknowledge the difficulty of the work and celebrate the team's positive impact. By making wellness an open and frequent topic of conversation, they create an environment where caring for one's mental health is seen not as a liability, but as a core professional responsibility. The human cost of content moderation is real and significant, but it does not have to be inevitable.

CHAPTER TWENTY-ONE: Measuring the Success of Your Moderation Efforts

For many organizations, the content moderation team operates like the engine room of a great ocean liner: essential, noisy, and almost completely invisible to the passengers on the upper decks until something goes catastrophically wrong. This invisibility creates a persistent challenge. How do you demonstrate the value of a function whose greatest successes are non-events—the crises that were averted, the flame wars that never erupted, the illegal content that never saw the light of day? Without a clear framework for measurement, moderation can be perceived as a pure "cost center," a necessary but unglamorous expense on a spreadsheet. To justify its budget, to advocate for resources, and to prove its vital contribution to the health of the community and the business, a moderation team must learn to speak the language of data.

Measuring the success of moderation is not about slapping a few numbers on a chart. It is about transforming the abstract goal of "community health" into a set of concrete, quantifiable Key Performance Indicators (KPIs). It is the process of building a dashboard that serves as a diagnostic tool for the community's well-being and a report card for the team's performance. This data-driven approach moves the conversation with stakeholders from subjective anecdotes ("the forums feel a lot less toxic lately") to objective facts ("our new moderation strategy has led to a 30% decrease in user reports of harassment"). This chapter will provide a blueprint for what to measure, how to measure it, and how to use that data to tell a compelling story about the value of your work.

The first step is to recognize that not all metrics are created equal. They generally fall into two broad categories: efficiency metrics and effectiveness metrics. Efficiency metrics measure the "how" of your operation. They are about speed, volume, and resources. How much work is the team doing, and how fast are they doing it? These metrics are crucial for managing staffing, optimizing workflows, and understanding the operational load. Effectiveness metrics, on the other hand, measure the "why." They are about quality, impact, and outcomes. Is the work the team is doing actually making a difference? Is the community becoming a safer and more positive place as a result of their efforts? A successful measurement framework must track both, as efficiency without effectiveness is just a fast way to make poor decisions.

Let's begin with the efficiency metrics, as they are often the easiest to track and form the foundation of your operational awareness. The most basic of these is **Queue Volume**. This is the total number of items—reported posts, flagged comments, new user accounts—that require a moderator's review in a given period. Tracking this metric over time is essential for resource planning. A sudden, sustained increase in queue volume is a clear signal that your current staffing levels may be insufficient to handle the load. Analyzing the sources of this volume is also critical. Is 80% of your queue coming from a single, poorly designed feature? That is a powerful, data-backed argument to take to the product team.

Once you know how much work is coming in, the next question is how quickly you are handling it. **Time to Action (TTA)**, sometimes called Time to First Response, measures the average time that elapses between a piece of content being reported and a moderator taking the first action on it. This is a direct measure of your team's responsiveness and a key indicator of the user experience. A low TTA means that harmful content is being removed quickly, minimizing its potential to damage the community. A long TTA means that reported content is festering, making the community feel neglected and unsafe. Tracking this metric by time of day or day of the week can reveal gaps in your moderation coverage that need to be filled.

While TTA measures the speed of response, **Handle Time** measures the speed of resolution. This is the average time it takes a moderator to complete a single case, from opening the ticket to logging the final action. This metric helps you understand the complexity of your workflow. For example, if you find that handle time for harassment cases is five times longer than for spam cases, it indicates that harassment investigations are more complex and require more of your team's resources. This insight can inform both training priorities and staffing models.

Combining these metrics gives you a measure of **Moderator Throughput**, which is the number of items a moderator can handle per hour or per shift. This is a core metric for building a staffing model that can keep pace with your queue volume. However, it is also one of the most dangerous metrics if used improperly. An overemphasis on throughput can lead to the "quota trap," where moderators feel pressured to hit a certain number of actions per hour. This incentivizes speed above all else, which can lead to rushed judgments, inconsistent decisions, and a dramatic decrease in the quality of moderation. Throughput is a valuable capacity planning tool, but it must always be balanced against the far more important metrics of effectiveness.

Effectiveness metrics are what separate a busy moderation team from a successful one. They measure the quality and the impact of the team's work. The single most important effectiveness metric is **Moderator Accuracy**, often measured as a Quality Assurance (QA) score. This is the percentage of a moderator's decisions that correctly applied the internal policies. An action is "correct" if it is the action that the official handbook and precedents say should have been taken. A 95% accuracy score means that, out of 100 decisions, 95 were consistent with the established rules.

Measuring accuracy requires a formal QA program. This typically involves a senior moderator, a team lead, or a dedicated QA specialist reviewing a random sample of each moderator's completed cases each week. The reviewer grades each decision against a detailed rubric. Was the correct rule cited? Was the correct action taken? Was the templated message used correctly? This process is not just about catching errors; it is the primary feedback loop for coaching and training. A low accuracy score for a specific moderator might indicate the need for one-on-one coaching. If the entire team is consistently making the same mistake on a certain type of case, it is a clear sign that the policy itself is confusing and needs to be clarified for everyone.

Another powerful set of effectiveness metrics can be derived from your appeals process. The **Appeal Rate** is the percentage of moderation decisions that are formally appealed by users. While some appeals are inevitable, a high or rising appeal rate can be a red flag. It may suggest that users do not understand the rules, that they perceive the enforcement to be unfair, or that the process for communicating a decision is unclear.

Even more telling is the **Overturn Rate**. This is the percentage of appeals that result in the original moderation decision being reversed. A high overturn rate is a serious problem. It means that, upon second review, your own team is finding that its initial decisions were incorrect. This is a direct and unambiguous indicator of low first-pass accuracy and inconsistency within the team. The goal should always be to get the decision right the first time, and the overturn rate is the ultimate measure of whether you are achieving that goal.

The gold standard for measuring moderation's impact, particularly for large platforms, is the **Prevalence of Violating Content (VVC)**. This metric seeks to answer the ultimate question: how much bad stuff are our users actually seeing? Instead of just measuring the work the team is doing (the number of items removed), VVC measures the content that is missed. It is typically calculated by taking a statistically significant, random sample of all content on the platform (including content that was never reported) and having a team of expert auditors review it against the policies. The result is an estimate of the percentage of all content views that are views of material that violates the rules.

Driving down VVC is the ultimate goal of a scaled moderation system. It is a holistic measure that reflects the effectiveness of everything from your proactive AI filters to your reactive human review teams. A decrease in VVC is a direct, quantifiable reduction in the harm users are exposed to on your platform. While complex to measure and typically reserved for larger organizations, the concept behind VVC is a useful guiding principle for any team. The goal is not just to close tickets; it is to reduce the amount of harm the community experiences.

Beyond the internal metrics of the moderation team, a mature measurement framework also incorporates a set of **Community Health Metrics**. These indicators measure the overall state of the community and can be used to correlate moderation efforts with positive user outcomes. **User Trust & Safety Sentiment** is a key example. This is typically measured through regular user surveys that ask direct questions like, "On a scale of 1 to 5, how safe do you feel from harassment in this community?" or "How confident are you that reported content will be handled appropriately?" A positive trend in these survey results is a powerful indicator that your moderation efforts are having the desired effect on user perception.

The **Recidivism Rate** is a behavioral metric that measures the effectiveness of your enforcement actions. It asks: what percentage of users who receive a warning or a temporary suspension go on to violate the rules again within a specific time frame? A low recidivism rate suggests that your penalties are acting as an effective deterrent and that your educational warnings are successfully correcting user behavior. A high rate might suggest that your penalties are not severe enough or that your communication is not clear.

Finally, a savvy community team can tie its moderation metrics directly to core business objectives. This is how you prove that moderation is not a cost center, but a value driver. This involves looking for correlations between moderation activities and key business metrics like **User Retention** and **Engagement**. For example, you might analyze the behavior of two cohorts of new users: one that joined a sub-community with very active, fast moderation and another that joined a sub-community with slower, less consistent moderation. If you can demonstrate that the new users in the well-moderated space have a higher 30-day retention rate, you have just drawn a direct, data-backed line between the investment in moderation and the business goal of retaining users.

Once you have this data, it is useless if it stays locked in a spreadsheet. It must be used to tell a story. This means creating a reporting cadence that serves different audiences. The moderation team itself might need a real-time operational dashboard and a daily report to manage the queue and spot immediate problems. Team leads might need a weekly report to track moderator performance and identify coaching opportunities. Senior leadership and other stakeholders need a condensed, high-level monthly or quarterly report that focuses on the big picture: the long-term trends in community health, the proven ROI of moderation efforts, and the strategic recommendations for future investments.

When presenting this data, always focus on the narrative. Do not just show a chart where Time to Action has decreased. Explain the story behind it: "In Q2, we added two moderators to the weekend shift. As you can see from this chart, this investment allowed us to reduce our average weekend TTA by 60%, bringing it in line with our weekday performance and ensuring a more consistent user experience." This is how you translate operational data into a language that budget holders and executives can understand and support.

As you build your measurement program, there are several common pitfalls to avoid. The first, as mentioned earlier, is the quota trap. Never let productivity metrics like Handle Time or Throughput become the primary measure of a moderator's performance. This will inevitably burn out your team and destroy the quality of their work. Accuracy must always be the north star.

The second pitfall is focusing on "vanity metrics." These are numbers that are easy to measure and often look impressive but do not actually signify success. The total "number of accounts banned," for instance, is a classic vanity metric. A high number of bans might seem like the team is being decisive, but it could also be a sign of a massive spam attack or a failure to correct user behavior at an earlier stage. Success is not banning more people; success is creating an environment where fewer people need to be banned.

Finally, remember that quantitative data tells you the "what," but it does not always tell you the "why." A sudden spike in reports of a certain kind is a valuable signal, but it is the qualitative insights from your moderators—the boots-on-the-ground intelligence—that will explain the context behind that spike. The best measurement programs blend this quantitative data with qualitative feedback from both the moderation team and the community itself, creating a holistic, three-dimensional view of the community's health. By embracing a culture of measurement, a moderation team can step out of the engine room and take its rightful place on the bridge, using data to navigate the community toward a safer, healthier, and more valuable future.

CHAPTER TWENTY-TWO: Transparency in Moderation: Communicating with Your Community

In the architecture of a healthy online community, trust is the load-bearing wall. When it crumbles, the entire structure is at risk of collapse. While consistent enforcement and fair rules are the bricks and mortar of this wall, the cement that binds them together is transparency. Transparency in moderation is the practice of communicating openly with the community about the rules, the enforcement actions, and the philosophies that guide the management of the space. It is the deliberate act of pulling back the curtain on the moderation process, transforming it from an opaque, mysterious "black box" into a system that users can understand, scrutinize, and, ultimately, trust.

This is not a call for absolute or radical transparency. A moderator's work involves sensitive user data and confidential security procedures that must remain private. Rather, the goal is strategic transparency. It is a commitment to explaining the "why" behind the "what." It is the difference between a sign that simply says "No Trespassing" and one that says "No Trespassing: Danger of Falling Rocks." The first is a command; the second is a reasoned explanation that fosters understanding and encourages voluntary compliance. An opaque moderation system, where content vanishes and users are suspended without a clear explanation, breeds suspicion, resentment, and a pervasive sense that the rules are arbitrary and the moderators are biased. A transparent system, even when its decisions are unpopular, builds a foundation of legitimacy that is essential for long-term health.

This commitment to open communication is not merely an ethical ideal; it is a powerful tool with a host of practical benefits. First and foremost, it is the most effective way to build and maintain trust. When users see that a popular community member was sanctioned for the same rule violation as a newcomer, and they understand the reasoning behind the action, it reinforces their belief in the fairness of the system. This trust is the currency that moderators spend every time they have to make a difficult or unpopular call. Without it, every action is viewed through a lens of suspicion, and the moderation team is forced to constantly defend itself against accusations of corruption, censorship, and personal bias.

Transparency is also a powerful educational tool that improves community-wide compliance. When a user understands the logic behind a rule—for example, that the rule against low-effort "meme" posts in a support forum exists to keep the space focused and helpful for people in crisis—they are far more likely to respect and follow it. The rule is no longer an arbitrary restriction on their fun, but a logical standard that contributes to the community's shared purpose. This understanding ripples outward, empowering the community to engage in the kind of effective self-moderation discussed in a previous chapter. Members who understand the rules are better equipped to model correct behavior and to flag violations accurately.

Finally, a transparent process significantly reduces the moderator's workload. An unexplained action is an invitation for questions, arguments, and accusations. A single, well-explained decision, communicated clearly from the outset, can preempt dozens of follow-up messages and public arguments. It allows the moderator to spend less time defending past decisions and more time focusing on the present health of the community. It transforms the dynamic from a constant, adversarial debate into a more collaborative relationship, where the moderation team and the community are understood to be working toward the same goal.

The practice of transparency begins with the most basic but crucial document: the community guidelines. As established earlier, these guidelines must be clear, comprehensive, and easy to find. This is the foundational act of transparency, the public contract between the platform and its users. However, publishing the rules is only half the battle. The true test of transparency lies in how those rules are communicated during the course of day-to-day enforcement.

The primary venue for this communication is the direct, private message. When a moderator removes a piece of content or issues a warning, the first step should almost always be a private notification to the user involved. Publicly scolding a user is rarely productive; it is an act of shaming that often causes the user to become defensive and escalate the conflict. A private message, by contrast, provides a space for a direct, non-confrontational, and educational interaction.

A good moderation message is a model of impersonal clarity. It should never be emotional or judgmental. It must contain three key pieces of information. First, it must specify exactly which piece of content was actioned. Quoting the offending post or comment removes all ambiguity. Second, it must state which specific rule was violated, ideally with a direct link to the full text of that rule in the community guidelines. Third, it must clearly state the action that was taken (e.g., "your comment was removed," "you have received a formal warning," "your account has been temporarily suspended for 24 hours"). This simple, three-part structure—what you did, why it broke the rules, and what the consequence is— transforms the action from a personal judgment into a standard procedural matter.

While most communication should be private, there are times when a public action is necessary and appropriate. When an entire thread has devolved into a toxic mess, a moderator locking the thread needs to leave a final, public comment explaining why. A simple, "This thread is no longer productive and has been locked. As a reminder, personal attacks are not permitted in this community," serves to educate everyone who was reading along and makes it clear that the closure was a procedural act of sanitation, not an arbitrary act of censorship.

Another common and effective form of public transparency is the use of generic moderation notes. When a single comment is removed from a thread, a moderator can leave a simple placeholder like "[Comment removed by moderator for violating the community guidelines on personal attacks]." This has two benefits. It maintains the conversational flow for other readers, preventing the confusion that can arise when a comment in a chain simply vanishes. More importantly, it is a visible signal that moderation is active in the space, which can have a powerful deterrent effect on others and increase the community's sense of safety.

This leads to the question of a formal appeals process. A transparent community must acknowledge that its moderators are human and can make mistakes. Providing a clear, well-defined, and easily accessible channel for users to appeal a moderation decision is a critical safety valve. It is a powerful statement of a commitment to fairness. The process itself need not be complicated. A dedicated email address or a private contact form is often sufficient. The key is that the appeal should, whenever possible, be reviewed by a different person than the moderator who made the initial decision. This ensures a fresh and unbiased second look. The existence of a fair appeals process can, on its own, de-escalate many complaints, as it gives an aggrieved user a constructive outlet for their frustration.

For communities seeking a higher level of transparency, some have experimented with public moderation logs. In such a system, a public, read-only feed is created that logs every moderation action—every deleted post, every banned user—along with the reason for the action. The theoretical benefit is absolute accountability; anyone can scrutinize the work of the moderation team. In practice, however, this approach is fraught with peril. It can expose moderators to a staggering amount of harassment, as every single decision becomes the subject of endless public debate. It can also create a culture of "meta-drama," where the community spends more time arguing about moderation than it does discussing its actual topic. Furthermore, it can create serious privacy issues for the users being moderated. The risks often outweigh the benefits, and this level of transparency is generally not recommended for most communities.

A far more scalable and effective model for high-level transparency is the periodic **Transparency Report**. This is a practice pioneered by large social media platforms that can be adapted for communities of almost any size. Instead of detailing every individual action, a transparency report provides aggregate data on moderation activity over a specific period, such as a quarter or a year. This report is a public statement from the community leadership, and it serves to illustrate the scale and nature of the moderation work that is happening behind the scenes.

A good transparency report might include data points such as the total volume of user reports received, the number of pieces of content removed, and a breakdown of those removals by policy category (e.g., 50% was spam, 20% was harassment, 10% was hate speech, etc.). It could also include the number of accounts that received a warning, a temporary suspension, or a permanent ban. Crucially, it should also include data on the appeals process, such as the total number of appeals received and the percentage of those appeals that resulted in an overturned decision. Publishing this data provides a powerful, high-level overview of the community's health and the moderation team's activities without getting bogged down in the drama of individual cases.

The final, and perhaps most important, arena for transparent communication is in the management of the rules themselves. Community guidelines should be treated as a living document, one that can and should evolve with the community. When a new type of disruptive behavior emerges that is not covered by the existing rules, the moderation team will need to create a new policy. This change must be communicated openly and proactively to the community. A public announcement should be made explaining the new rule, the rationale behind why it is necessary, and the date on which it will go into effect. This process of public consultation can be invaluable. Posting a draft of a new rule and soliciting community feedback before it is enacted can help identify unforeseen consequences and increases user buy-in, making the final rule feel like a community decision rather than a top-down edict.

Of course, there are necessary limits to transparency. No moderation team can be transparent about the specific inner workings of its anti-spam or anti-fraud tools, as doing so would simply provide a roadmap for malicious actors to evade them. Similarly, the details of an investigation involving credible threats or potential illegal activity that may be shared with law enforcement must remain strictly confidential. The safety and privacy of the moderators themselves is another critical boundary. It is often a wise policy for moderators to take public actions using a generic, shared "Moderation Team" account, rather than their personal accounts. This prevents every action from being associated with a specific individual, thereby reducing the risk of that individual becoming a target for personal harassment. The goal is to be transparent about the policies and processes, not to expose the people who carry them out.

Ultimately, the right level of transparency is a balance. It is a constant negotiation between the community's right to understand how it is being governed and the platform's need to protect the safety of its users, the privacy of its members, and the security of its operations. The guiding principle should always be to default to openness wherever possible. Every piece of information that can be shared without creating a direct security or privacy risk should be shared. This commitment to communication is not an optional extra; it is a core function of a healthy moderation system. It is the hard, continuous work of building the trust that allows a community not just to survive its conflicts, but to become stronger and more resilient because of them.

CHAPTER TWENTY-THREE: The Ethics of Content Moderation

The practice of content moderation is, at its heart, a series of judgments. It is a relentless, high-stakes process of drawing lines in the shifting sands of human expression. The preceding chapters have focused on the practicalities of this work: the laws that provide its framework, the tools that enable its execution, and the procedures that give it structure. But beneath this operational surface lies a turbulent and often uncharted ocean of ethical dilemmas. The law can tell a moderator what is legal, and the guidelines can tell them what is permitted, but neither can definitively answer the far more difficult question: what is right? This is the domain of ethics, the branch of philosophy concerned with moral principles. For a moderator, every action—from removing a comment to banning a user—is a moral decision with real consequences for individuals and the social fabric of the community.

The central, unavoidable ethical conflict that defines content moderation is the tension between two deeply held, and often incompatible, values: the commitment to free expression and the responsibility to ensure safety. Free expression is cherished as a cornerstone of open societies, the essential mechanism for challenging power, discovering truth, and enabling individual self-fulfillment. The ideal of a "marketplace of ideas," where all viewpoints can be aired and the best will naturally rise to the top, is a powerful and attractive one. In this view, the best cure for bad speech is more speech, not enforced silence. Any act of removing content can be seen as an act of censorship, a paternalistic decision that presumes a moderator knows better than the community what it should or should not see.

On the other side of this ethical scale is the profound responsibility to protect users from harm. An online space that permits unchecked harassment, hate speech, threats, and dangerous misinformation is not a thriving marketplace of ideas; it is a hostile and dangerous environment where the most vulnerable are silenced and driven away. The freedom of a user to post a death threat directly infringes upon the freedom of the target to exist safely in that space. In this view, the failure to moderate is not a noble defense of free speech, but an abdication of the basic duty of care owed to the community. Safety, proponents argue, is the precondition for any meaningful expression to occur. Without it, the conversation is inevitably dominated by the loudest, most aggressive, and most malicious voices.

This is not a simple problem with a tidy solution. It is a perpetual balancing act performed on a high wire, with no safety net. The core of the dilemma is that both sides are arguing from a place of legitimate moral concern. There is no universally accepted formula for how to weigh one person's freedom to speak against another person's freedom from harm. The "right" balance is a matter of constant, agonizing debate, both in society at large and within the private war rooms of every major platform. The ethical challenge for a moderator is that they are the ones who must execute this imperfect balance, making split-second judgment calls on ambiguous cases that philosophers could debate for a lifetime.

This immense responsibility places significant power in the hands of the moderator. Within the digital borders of their community, they are the police, the judiciary, and often the legislature, all rolled into one. This concentration of power raises profound ethical questions about neutrality and bias. A moderator is not a disembodied algorithm; they are a human being with their own life experiences, cultural background, political beliefs, and unconscious biases. The ideal of a perfectly neutral, objective moderator who applies the rules with the dispassionate precision of a machine is a useful fiction, but it is not a reality.

The ethical obligation, then, is not to achieve an impossible state of pure neutrality, but to actively recognize and mitigate the influence of one's own biases. This requires a rigorous commitment to self-awareness and procedural fairness. A moderator must constantly ask themselves: Am I applying this rule more harshly to a viewpoint I personally disagree with? Am I giving the benefit of the doubt to a user who is part of my social in-group? This is why a well-documented handbook with clear precedents is so vital; it acts as an external check on a moderator's internal inclinations. The ethical moderator is one who strives to be a fair arbiter of the community's established rules, not a champion for their own personal worldview.

This challenge is magnified by the ambiguity of the very concept of "harm." Most moderation decisions hinge on a judgment that a piece of content is, in some way, harmful. But the definition of harm is incredibly elastic. The law has a relatively clear definition for specific harms like defamation or incitement to violence. But the vast majority of moderated content falls into a much grayer zone of psychological or emotional harm. Is a user who feels insulted by a political opinion "harmed"? What about a user who is distressed by seeing a heated but non-threatening argument?

The ethical dilemma lies in deciding where to draw the line. An overly broad definition of harm, where any content that causes subjective offense is removed, can lead to a sterile, sanitized environment where no meaningful debate can occur. This is the path to the "heckler's veto," where the most sensitive members of a community are effectively given the power to silence any speech they dislike simply by claiming it is harmful. Conversely, an overly narrow definition of harm, one that only acknowledges direct threats of physical violence, creates a space that is technically safe but psychologically brutal, permitting relentless bullying and harassment that can cause severe and lasting emotional damage.

The choice of where to place this threshold is a reflection of the community's core values. A rough-and-tumble political debate forum will have a much higher tolerance for aggressive language than a support group for trauma survivors. The ethical imperative is for this definition of harm to be established and communicated with as much clarity as possible, so that members can make an informed choice about whether the community's standards align with their own.

Even with a clear definition, the principle of consistency presents its own ethical puzzles. A core tenet of fairness is that the rules should apply equally to everyone. In theory, this is simple. In practice, it is a minefield. What is the ethical course of action when a strict, consistent application of a minor rule would require you to ban a beloved, long-standing member who has contributed immense value to the community over many years? Is it more just to follow the letter of the law, demonstrating absolute consistency, or to make an exception, preserving a valuable community asset at the cost of appearing to play favorites?

This is a classic clash between two major schools of ethical thought. A deontological approach, focused on duties and rules, would argue that the rule must be followed, no matter the outcome. The fairness of the system itself is the highest good, and exceptions, no matter how well-intentioned, corrode the trust that the system depends on. A consequentialist approach, focused on outcomes, would argue that the most ethical action is the one that produces the best result. In this view, if banning the veteran member would do more harm to the community's health and morale than the original infraction did, then making a discretionary exception is the more ethical choice. There is no easy answer, and moderators are often forced to navigate this treacherous terrain, weighing the value of the rule against the value of the person.

The rise of AI and automation introduces a new and deeply complex layer to the ethical landscape. The sheer scale of modern platforms makes some degree of automation a necessity, but this reliance on algorithms to make decisions about human speech is laden with moral risk. The most significant of these is the problem of algorithmic bias. A machine learning model is not objective; it is a reflection of the data on which it was trained. If that data, which is often labeled by human reviewers, contains the same societal biases that exist in the real world, the AI will learn, codify, and perpetuate those biases at a massive, inhuman scale.

For example, if an AI is trained on a dataset where comments written in African American Vernacular English (AAVE) were disproportionately flagged as "toxic" by reviewers, it will learn to associate that dialect with toxicity. The result is a system that might automatically and unfairly penalize members of a specific demographic group, not because of any malicious intent, but because of the baked-in biases of its creators and its training data. This raises a crucial question of accountability. When a biased algorithm wrongfully suspends a user, who is morally responsible? Is it the engineer who built the model, the company that deployed it, or the human reviewers who labeled the original data? The diffusion of responsibility in these complex socio-technical systems makes true accountability incredibly difficult to pinpoint.

Furthermore, the very nature of automation can create a sense of moral detachment. When a human moderator makes a decision to remove a piece of content, they are directly confronted with the moral weight of that choice. An automated system, by contrast, operates at a distance, executing millions of "moderation actions" per hour without any awareness of the human context or the consequences of its decisions. This can create an ethical blind spot for the organizations that rely on these systems, allowing them to enforce policies at a scale that would be impossible, and perhaps unconscionable, if every decision had to be filtered through the conscience of a human being.

This speaks to the broader ethical responsibilities of the platforms themselves. A for-profit company that hosts a community is not a neutral public square; it is a private entity with its own commercial interests. This creates an inherent and powerful ethical conflict. Very often, the content that is most outrageous, most divisive, and most emotionally charged is also the most engaging. It generates the most clicks, comments, and shares, which in turn generates the most user data and the most advertising revenue. A platform, therefore, can find itself in the ethically compromised position of being financially incentivized to tolerate, and even algorithmically amplify, the very content that its own moderation teams are working to contain.

The decision of how much to invest in moderation is, itself, an ethical one. Every dollar spent on hiring and supporting trust and safety professionals is a dollar that does not go to product development or shareholder profits. The chronic under-resourcing of moderation teams on many platforms is not just a business decision; it is a moral choice that prioritizes financial gain over the well-being of the platform's users and its own employees.

This leads to the final, and perhaps most personal, ethical obligation: the duty of care that a platform owes to its moderators. Is it ethical to build a business model that requires human beings to spend their days immersed in a relentless stream of hate, violence, and trauma? Chapter Twenty explored the devastating personal cost of this work. The ethical dimension of this problem asks what a company is morally obligated to do in response. Providing robust, proactive, and fully-funded mental health support is not just a matter of good management or employee benefits; it is a fundamental ethical requirement for any organization that profits from this psychologically hazardous labor. To do otherwise is to treat its moderators as disposable components in a machine, a practice that is both unsustainable and morally indefensible.

The ethics of content moderation are not about finding a perfect, universal rulebook. No such book exists. Instead, it is about cultivating a deep and abiding sense of moral inquiry. It is the practice of constantly questioning the assumptions behind the rules, being aware of the immense power one wields, and recognizing the profound human impact of every decision. It is the humble acknowledgment that the work is performed in a world of gray areas, where the goal is not to achieve a perfect outcome, but to consistently and conscientiously strive for the lesser of two harms.

CHAPTER TWENTY-FOUR: Cross-Platform and Cross-Cultural Moderation Challenges

For a community in its infancy, the world is often a simple and self-contained place. It exists on a single platform, is governed by a single set of rules, and its members are drawn from a relatively homogenous cultural background. The challenges of moderation, while significant, are at least contained within these well-defined borders. But the internet does not respect borders. A successful community will inevitably spill over its original container, establishing outposts on new platforms and attracting members from every corner of the globe. This expansion is a sign of vitality, but it is also the point at which the neat and tidy practice of moderation collides with the chaotic, fragmented, and wonderfully complex reality of the global village.

The challenges of this new landscape are twofold. First is the cross-platform problem: how do you maintain a consistent culture and a coherent set of rules when your community is scattered across a dozen different services, each with its own tools, features, and limitations? Second is the far more profound cross-cultural problem: how do you apply a single standard of conduct to a global user base that speaks hundreds of different languages and adheres to thousands of different social norms? These are not theoretical edge cases; for any community of scale, they are the central, defining challenges of modern moderation.

Let's first consider the cross-platform dilemma. It is a rare community today that exists solely on a single, self-hosted forum. A more typical "community ecosystem" might consist of a central website, a bustling Discord server for real-time chat, a subreddit for broader outreach, and a collection of social media accounts on platforms like X (formerly Twitter) or Instagram for announcements and engagement. This distributed presence is excellent for meeting users where they are, but it is a logistical nightmare from a moderation perspective. The core of the problem is the fragmentation of both user identity and moderator authority.

A user who is a model citizen on the main forum might be a relentless troll on the associated Discord server. This creates an immediate enforcement paradox. If you ban them from the Discord, should that ban extend to the forum where they have a positive track record? The answer depends entirely on the community's overarching policy, a policy that must be explicitly defined. A failure to do so leads to an inconsistent and confusing user experience, where a user's reputation and status are reset every time they move from one platform to another. Tracking these fragmented identities is a challenge in itself. While some users maintain the same username everywhere, many do not, requiring moderators to become digital detectives to connect a pattern of malicious behavior back to a single individual.

This problem is compounded by the wild inconsistency of the tools available on each platform. The moderation dashboard on a self-hosted forum might be a powerful and granular tool, allowing for detailed user notes, custom suspension lengths, and a full audit log. The tools provided by a platform like Discord are different, while the moderation options on Reddit are different again. A moderator on a cross-platform team cannot just learn one system; they must become a multilingual expert in a half-dozen different, and often clunky, backend interfaces. A simple action, like issuing a standardized warning, might require three different workflows on three different platforms. This operational friction slows down response times and makes consistent enforcement a monumental chore.

Perhaps the greatest cross-platform challenge is the "platform of platforms" problem. When your community exists as a Facebook Group or a subreddit, you are not the ultimate landlord of your own space. You are a tenant, subject to the rules of the master platform. This creates a dual-authority structure. Your community has its own guidelines, but it is also subject to the overarching Terms of Service of Facebook or the Content Policy of Reddit. A piece of content might be perfectly acceptable under your community's rules—perhaps a piece of edgy but relevant satire—but could be a clear violation of the host platform's policy on harassment or hate speech.

In these situations, the moderator's hands are tied. They must enforce the host platform's rules, even if they conflict with their own community's culture, or risk having their entire community shut down. This can create deep resentment among members who feel that the local moderators are betraying the community's values, when in fact they are simply complying with a non-negotiable directive from a higher power. This is the precarious reality of building a community on rented land; you are always subject to the whims of the property owner.

This fragmentation creates a constant communication challenge. How do you ensure that every member of the community, regardless of which platform they primarily use, is aware of a major rule change or a new community event? A pinned post on the forum is invisible to someone who only uses the Discord server. An announcement in a specific Discord channel will be missed by the subreddit regulars. Maintaining a consistent message across these silos requires a disciplined, multi-channel communication strategy. Many communities solve this by establishing a "single source of truth"—a central website or blog where all official rules and announcements are posted—and then using all other platforms to point back to this canonical source.

If the cross-platform challenge is a matter of technology and logistics, the cross-cultural challenge is a far deeper and more human problem. It stems from a simple, unavoidable fact: the internet is global, but context is local. A moderation policy written in a conference room in California, based on Western, English-speaking social norms, will inevitably fail when it is applied without modification to a user in Tokyo, Cairo, or São Paulo. The very words and symbols that form the basis of moderation do not have a fixed, universal meaning.

The most immediate barrier is, of course, language. A moderation team that only speaks English is functionally blind to the content being posted in Spanish, Mandarin, Hindi, or any of the thousands of other languages spoken by a global user base. This forces a reliance on two imperfect solutions: hiring a multilingual moderation team or using automated translation tools. Building a global team is the better but more expensive option. Machine translation, while constantly improving, is notoriously bad at capturing the nuance, slang, and cultural subtext that is essential for accurate moderation. A literal translation can easily miss a sarcastic tone, a coded slur, or a pop culture reference, leading the moderator to make a decision based on incomplete and often misleading information.

Even with a perfect translation, the problem of cultural context remains. Words are more than their dictionary definitions; they are vessels of cultural meaning. A term that is a harmless piece of slang in one country can be a deeply offensive pejorative in another, even among countries that share the same language. The American "c-word" is a prime example; while it is one of the most offensive terms in American English, it is used with far more casual and even jocular frequency in British and Australian English. A moderator without this cultural context, applying a single, global profanity filter, will end up over-moderating entire regions.

This extends to non-verbal communication. Memes, images, and even emoji do not have universal meanings. A popular meme format in one part of the world might be completely inscrutable in another. A hand gesture that is innocuous in one culture can be a grave insult in a second and a political statement in a third. The "OK" hand sign, for instance, has in some contexts been co-opted as a symbol of white supremacy, a meaning that is entirely absent for the vast majority of people who use it. How is a moderator supposed to judge the intent of a user posting that symbol without knowing the specific subculture from which they are posting? The risk of misinterpretation is immense.

Beyond the meaning of individual words and symbols, different cultures have fundamentally different communication styles and social norms. What one culture considers to be healthy, direct debate, another might perceive as aggressive and disrespectful confrontation. What one culture views as polite deference to authority, another might see as a lack of critical thought. A universal guideline like "Be Respectful" is not a fixed standard; it is a mirror that reflects the cultural assumptions of the person reading it. A moderation team that does not account for this diversity will inevitably end up imposing the norms of its own dominant culture on the entire global community, creating an environment that can feel exclusionary and alienating to a significant portion of its user base.

This cultural relativism collides head-on with the legal and political realities of a fragmented world. As discussed in Chapter Eleven, the laws governing speech vary dramatically from one country to the next. Content that is legally protected political speech in the United States, such as Holocaust denial, is a criminal offense in Germany and several other European countries. A platform that operates globally is not subject to one set of laws, but to the laws of every country in which it has users.

This creates an almost impossible tightrope walk for policy makers and moderators. A truly global community policy must somehow navigate these conflicting legal requirements. A common approach is to adopt a "geo-gating" or "country-withheld" content model, where a piece of content that is illegal in a specific country is made invisible to users in that country but remains visible elsewhere. This allows the platform to comply with local laws without removing the content globally. However, this approach is often criticized as a form of censorship that allows authoritarian regimes to dictate what their citizens can see online. The ethical and political complexities are immense, and the moderator on the front lines is often the one tasked with executing these geopolitically sensitive decisions.

Navigating this maze of challenges requires a fundamental shift away from a one-size-fits-all approach to moderation. The first and most important strategy for dealing with cross-cultural issues is to build a diverse and globally representative moderation team. You cannot effectively moderate a community you do not understand.

Hiring moderators who are native speakers and residents of the regions they are responsible for is the single most effective way to acquire the necessary linguistic and cultural expertise. These moderators can not only handle reports in the local language, but they can also serve as invaluable cultural consultants, helping the central policy team understand local norms and avoid making culturally ignorant mistakes.

In place of a single, rigid set of global guidelines, a more flexible, tiered approach is often more effective. This involves creating a set of universal, foundational principles that apply to the entire community—such as a zero-tolerance policy for illegal content and credible threats of violence. Beneath this universal layer, the platform can then allow for the creation of region-specific or even language-specific community codes of conduct. These local addendums, often developed in consultation with the local community and enforced by local moderators, can provide more nuanced guidance on issues like profanity, humor, and communication styles that are specific to that culture.

When building AI and automation tools, this cultural awareness must be baked in from the beginning. A toxicity detection model trained exclusively on American English will perform poorly and unfairly when applied to conversations in India or Nigeria. Developing effective global AI requires a massive and ongoing investment in collecting and labeling diverse, multilingual, and region-specific training data. It also requires a recognition that for the most culturally nuanced issues, the AI's role should be to flag content for a culturally-aware human expert, not to make an automated decision on its own.

Ultimately, the challenges of moderating a cross-platform and cross-cultural community are a reflection of the internet itself: fragmented, complex, and deeply, irreducibly human. There are no easy answers or simple technological fixes. Success requires a commitment to building systems, teams, and policies that are as flexible, diverse, and context-aware as the global communities they are meant to serve. It is the difficult but essential work of transforming a collection of disparate digital spaces into a truly global and inclusive home.

CHAPTER TWENTY-FIVE: The Future of Online Community Moderation

The practice of online community moderation has always been a story of adaptation. From the informal "netiquette" of the early Usenet days to the global, AI-powered trust and safety operations of today, moderators have constantly evolved their tools and tactics to keep pace with the relentless innovation of the internet itself. This final chapter is not a conclusion, but a forecast. The forces of technological advancement, regulatory pressure, and shifting user expectations are converging to shape a future for moderation that will be profoundly different from its past. The core mission—fostering safe and constructive spaces—will remain the same, but the methods for achieving it are on the verge of a radical transformation. The future of moderation will be more predictive, more personalized, more regulated, and will demand a new and more sophisticated set of skills from its human practitioners.

The most significant technological shift is the move from a reactive to a proactive, and even predictive, model of moderation. For most of its history, moderation has been an act of digital archaeology, sifting through the remains of a conversation to find and remove the pieces that broke the rules. The future lies in identifying and mitigating harm before it has a chance to fully manifest. Artificial intelligence is at the heart of this transition, moving beyond simple content analysis to sophisticated behavioral analysis. Future systems will not just ask, "Does this comment contain a slur?" but will ask, "Does this user's pattern of activity suggest they are here to cause trouble?"

This predictive capability is powered by machine learning models that analyze behavioral signals, not just words. These systems can identify accounts that are created at an unusual velocity, that immediately start following a large number of controversial figures, or that engage in repetitive, non-conversational posting patterns. This allows for the detection of "inauthentic behavior" associated with spam networks, disinformation campaigns, and coordinated harassment mobs. By flagging these accounts based on their behavior, platforms can intervene before they have a chance to launch their payload of toxic content. This is the digital equivalent of spotting a known arsonist loitering near a dry forest with a can of gasoline.

This extends to the health of conversations themselves. AI models are being developed to assign a "health score" to a discussion thread in real-time. By analyzing factors like the rate of replies, the use of absolutist language, the prevalence of ad hominem arguments, and the sentiment of the conversation, the system can flag a thread that is on the verge of becoming toxic. This acts as an early warning system for human moderators, allowing them to proactively step into a discussion with a gentle reminder or a de-escalation technique before it devolves into a full-blown flame war. It transforms the moderator from a firefighter into a fire marshal, capable of identifying and mitigating risks before the blaze begins.

This predictive power, however, walks a fine ethical line. The concept of "pre-crime," where users are sanctioned for actions they have not yet taken but are predicted to take, is a dystopian prospect. A user flagged for "inauthentic behavior" may simply be an eccentric newcomer who does not yet understand the community's norms. The ethical implementation of these predictive tools will require a system of checks and balances, with the AI serving to alert and inform human judgment, not to replace it. The decision to act will still rest with a person, but that person will be armed with a new level of foresight.

At the same time that AI is getting better at seeing the big picture, it is also becoming far more adept at understanding the small one. The era of one-size-fits-all, generic toxicity models is coming to an end. The future lies in hyper-personalization and deep contextual awareness. Large language models (LLMs) are the driving force behind this revolution. These models, trained on vast swathes of the internet, possess an unprecedented ability to understand the nuances of human language, including slang, sarcasm, and intricate cultural references.

This allows for the creation of moderation AI that is tailored to the specific micro-culture of a single community. An AI can be fine-tuned on a community's own history, learning its inside jokes and its specific definitions of acceptable behavior. It can learn that in a particular gaming community, the phrase "get wrecked" is a form of playful banter, while in a mental health support group, it would be a cruel and unacceptable insult. This contextual understanding will dramatically reduce the number of false positives that frustrate users and will allow for a far more nuanced and culturally-attuned application of the rules.

These advanced models will also revolutionize the educational component of moderation. Instead of a user receiving a cold, templated message stating that their post was removed for "harassment," a future system powered by an LLM could provide a detailed and personalized explanation. The AI could generate a message like, "Your recent comment was removed because it used the phrase 'you people,' which, in the context of this discussion about immigration, can be interpreted as a dehumanizing generalization. Our goal is to encourage debate about ideas, not to make broad attacks on groups of people. Please review our policy on respectful conversation here." This automates the painstaking work of explaining the "why," freeing human moderators to handle the most complex cases.

As the technology of moderation evolves, so too do the spaces that require it. The flat, text-based world of forums and social media feeds is rapidly being augmented by new, immersive, and decentralized environments, each presenting a unique and formidable moderation challenge. The rise of the metaverse and other persistent, 3D virtual worlds forces a complete rethinking of what "content" even is. In these spaces, harm can be communicated not just through text or images, but through invasive body language, threatening gestures, or the violation of personal space. How do you moderate a user who is silently and menacingly following another user's avatar through a virtual plaza? How do you create a reporting system for an offensive symbol drawn in the air with a virtual tool that disappears seconds later?

Moderating these real-time, ephemeral interactions will require a new class of tools. It will likely involve a combination of automated behavioral analysis that can detect aggressive movement patterns, and user-activated recording tools that can capture the last thirty seconds of an interaction to be submitted as evidence. Human moderators may need to patrol these virtual spaces as avatars themselves, acting as a visible presence to deter bad behavior, much like a police officer walking a beat. The logistical and psychological challenges of moderating these embodied, synchronous environments are immense.

Simultaneously, a growing movement toward decentralized social media, often called the "fediverse," presents a structural challenge to the very idea of centralized moderation. On platforms like Mastodon, the network is not a single, corporate-owned entity, but a collection of thousands of independent, interconnected servers, or "instances." Each instance is run by its own administrator, who sets their own rules. This creates a distributed model of moderation, where the first line of defense is the local admin. Users can choose an instance whose moderation philosophy aligns with their own.

This model offers a powerful alternative to the dominance of a few large platforms, but it creates complex, new problems. Harassment can become "federated," where a user on a poorly moderated instance can send a flood of abuse to a user on a well-moderated one. The only recourse for the victim's admin is to "defederate," or completely block all communication from the offending server, effectively cutting off an entire community because of the actions of a few. This raises difficult questions about collective responsibility and creates the potential for the internet to fragment into isolated, ideologically-opposed blocs. In this decentralized world, the moderator is not an employee of a global corporation, but often a volunteer administrator, a diplomat, and a treaty negotiator, all at once.

This technological and structural evolution is not happening in a vacuum. It is occurring alongside a seismic shift in the legal and regulatory landscape. The era of self-regulation, exemplified by the broad legal shield of Section 230 in the United States, is drawing to a close. Around the world, governments are moving decisively toward a model of co-regulation, where platforms are no longer left to police themselves but are subject to a growing list of legal obligations. The European Union's Digital Services Act (DSA) is the most comprehensive blueprint for this new reality.

The DSA and similar laws emerging globally will fundamentally reshape the operational requirements for moderation teams. They will mandate a new level of transparency, legally requiring platforms to provide clear explanations to users for every piece of content that is removed. They will codify the right to a robust and functional appeals process. They will require large platforms to publish detailed transparency reports, to submit to independent audits, and to conduct thorough "systemic risk assessments." This last requirement is the most profound. Regulators are no longer just concerned with individual bad posts; they are demanding that platforms analyze and mitigate the risks that are inherent in the very design of their systems. The question is no longer just, "How quickly did you remove the hate speech?" but, "How did your recommendation algorithm end up amplifying that hate speech to millions of people in the first place?"

This shifts the work of a senior moderation professional from a purely operational function to a core part of the product development lifecycle. The Trust & Safety team of the future will not just be cleaning up messes at the end of the pipeline; they will be at the design table from the very beginning, acting as internal consultants to ensure that new features are built with safety and risk mitigation in mind. This is the concept of "Safety by Design," a proactive approach that seeks to prevent harm rather than simply reacting to it.

This complex and demanding new environment will necessitate a transformation in the role and skills of the human moderator. The high-volume, frontline work of reviewing obvious spam and clear-cut violations will become almost entirely automated. The human moderator of the future will be a highly-skilled knowledge worker, not a digital content screener. Their role will shift to that of the "human-in-the-loop," the expert arbiter who handles the complex cases that the AI cannot solve.

The moderator of the future will be an AI trainer, providing the nuanced feedback that is necessary to make the automated systems smarter. They will be a complex investigator, piecing together evidence from multiple sources to uncover sophisticated, coordinated abuse networks. They will be an appeals judge, providing a thoughtful and empathetic second look at the decisions made by the automated systems. They will be a policy expert, using their on-the-ground knowledge to help shape the rules that govern the community. This will require a new skill set, one that blends deep cultural and linguistic knowledge with data analysis skills and a sophisticated understanding of how socio-technical systems work.

This evolution will, and must, be accompanied by a growing professionalization of the field. The recognition of the profound psychological toll of the work, as detailed in Chapter Twenty, is leading to a greater demand for better support, higher pay, and clearer career paths. The job of a trust and safety professional will be increasingly seen not as an entry-level customer support role, but as a specialized and critical function, akin to a paralegal or an intelligence analyst. The long-term health of the internet depends on the ability to attract and retain talented, resilient, and well-supported professionals to do this essential work.

Finally, the future of moderation will likely see a move beyond the simple, punitive models of the past. The traditional toolkit of warnings, suspensions, and bans is a blunt instrument. While necessary for dealing with malicious actors, it is often ineffective for correcting the behavior of well-intentioned users who simply make mistakes. The future lies in developing more sophisticated and nuanced systems of user management, some of which are inspired by the real-world concept of restorative justice.

This could involve the use of "educational friction." Imagine a user typing a comment that an AI flags as potentially harassing. Instead of simply blocking the comment after it is posted, the system could intervene before the fact, showing a pop-up that says, "Are you sure you want to post this? Comments that use this kind of language are often perceived as personal attacks. Please take a moment to review our guidelines." This small moment of friction, this "nudge," can be surprisingly effective at causing a user to reconsider and rephrase their comment, preventing the harm from ever occurring.

Other approaches focus on giving users more granular control over their own experience, effectively allowing them to create personalized layers of moderation. A user might be given the ability to set their own keyword filters, to automatically collapse comments from new or low-reputation accounts, or to opt out of seeing threads on certain sensitive topics. This empowers users to curate a safer and more pleasant environment for themselves, reducing the burden on the central moderation team to create a single experience that satisfies everyone.

The journey of online community moderation is one of constant learning and unceasing change. The challenges on the horizon—immersive virtual worlds, decentralized networks, increasingly sophisticated malicious actors—are more complex than anything the field has faced before. Yet, the tools for meeting these challenges—context-aware AI, data-driven insights, a global community of dedicated professionals—are also more powerful than ever. The core task remains a deeply human one: the delicate and essential work of balancing freedom with safety, enabling conversation, and building the resilient, inclusive, and trustworthy communities that will shape the future of our digital world.

www.ingramcontent.com/pod-product-compliance
Lightning Source LLC
LaVergne TN
LVHW052059060326
832903LV00061B/3625